Girl, have I got good news for you

thelma wells

W PUBLISHING GROUP
A Division of Thomas Nelson Publishers
Since 1798

www.wpublishinggroup.com

Published in Nashville, Tennessee, by Thomas Nelson, Inc.

Published in association with the literary agency of Alive Communications, 1465 Kelly Johnson Blvd., Suite 320, Colorado Springs, CO 80920.

Scripture quotations noted NKJV are from THE NEW KING JAMES VERSION. Copyright © 1979, 1980, 1982, Thomas Nelson, Inc., Publishers.

Scripture quotations noted NIV are from the HOLY BIBLE: NEW INTERNATIONAL VERSION®. Copyright © 1973, 1978, 1984 by International Bible Society. Used by permission of Zondervan Publishing House. All rights reserved.

Scripture quotations noted KJV are from the KING JAMES VERSION.

Library of Congress Cataloging-in-Publication Data

ISBN 0-8499-4473-2 (sc)
ISBN 0-7852-7547-9 (hc)

Printed in the United States of America

04 05 06 07 08 PHX 6 5 4 3 2

Contents

Contents

Acknowledgments

This book is made possible by the trust, support, and encouragement of the Thomas Nelson Publishing family.

Rolf Zettersten, publisher

Dr. Victor Oliver, president, Oliver Nelson Books

Janet Thoma, vice president, Janet Thoma Books

Cindy Blades, managing editor

What would I do without my literary agent, Kathryn Yanni; my editor, Traci Mullins; my producer, confidante, and daughter, Vikki Wells; and my loving husband and business manager, George Wells? I would be without the best team of Christian professionals anyone could ask for.

Judy Skelton invested hours of prayer, energy, and skill to help make this book a reality. God bless you, Judy!

An extra special thanks goes to the thousands of ladies in our country who had enough confidence in me to trust me with their personal situations. Because of their honesty and vulnerability, they have provided a forum for women in similar situations to dialogue through the pages of this book.

Behind all the work I do are my husband, George, and our children, George F. Wells and Lesa Cohen. My son's constant inspiration, compliments, and bear hugs push me onward. Lesa is there constantly, praying and offering tidbits of power from the Word of God. This mother counts her children and husband as "Blessed!" Thank you all for your constant faith in me.

From the Heart,
Thelma Wells
BEE Blessed!

Introduction

Girl, Have I Got Good News for You

Therefore, brothers, since we have confidence to enter the Most Holy Place by the blood of Jesus, by a new and living way opened for us through the curtain, that is, his body, and since we have a great priest over the house of God, let us draw near to God with a sincere heart in full assurance of faith, having our hearts sprinkled to cleanse us from a guilty conscience and having our bodies washed with pure water. Let us hold unswervingly to the hope we profess, for he who promised is faithful. And let us consider how we may spur one another on toward love and good deeds. Let us not give up meeting together, as some are in the habit of doing, but let us encourage one another—and all the more as you see the Day approaching.

—Hebrews 10:19–25 NIV

The apostle Paul's words sum up well the climate that has developed in the New Life Women of Faith conferences. When I started speaking for this movement in the summer of 1996, I had no idea what was in store for me. My five fellow speakers and I have had the privilege of touching the lives of many thousands of women across the United States as we've sought to encourage, inspire, influence, inform, and entertain.

All six of us speakers have different backgrounds, different life experiences, different denominations, different dress sizes, and different speaking styles, but we're bound together by a common denominator, *love*. Love for God, love for each other, and love for the people we meet week after week. Whether we are getting together with a small group or interacting with thousands, we have one basic goal in mind: to ignite a spark of joy, peace, hope, grace, love, and freedom in every person who will receive it.

Often this goal is a challenge to attain because, like us, women come to the conferences not only with social and cultural differences, but also with heartbreak and tribulations that confound our finite ability to handle them correctly and adequately. Over the past three years, I have kept a mental list of the hurts and concerns of the women who are in the meetings where I've ministered. Women talk to me face-to-face, E-mail, write, telephone, and send messages via their friends or family members asking for solutions or encouragement in their difficult situations.

In every interaction, I've prayed silently for understanding and wisdom. I sure am grateful that I don't have to know everything! I can go to the Source and get answers that are not only correct and adequate, but also completely foolproof when applied with persistence and in faith. I turn to the infinite, powerful Word of God. *And, Girl, does it have good news for you!*

In the pages ahead, I have looked to the holy Scriptures and the Holy Spirit within to offer direction and encouragement for what I've discovered to be some of the most common trials women face today. I hope you will find some help for your troubles as well as wisdom and encouragement to offer a hurting friend.

Jesus said, "In the world you will have tribulation; but be of good cheer" (John 16:33 NKJV). How outrageous! Be of good cheer when you have problems in your life? That doesn't make sense if you stop reading there. But if you believe the next statement, "I have overcome the world," it all makes sense. Jesus has the authority to declare that profound encouragement because He lived and died and rose again to make it true.

This is Your life, Jesus:

You were carried in the womb of an unwed, virgin teenager for nine months. You were born in a barn with horses, cows, chickens, and goats to greet You. Angels announced Your birth, proclaiming with joy that peace and goodwill had come to earth.

You went into exile in Egypt until baby boys were no longer

being killed by the Roman government. You learned the skill of carpentry from Your earthly father. You had other siblings to play with. You got hungry, thirsty, and dirty.

You were fascinated with Your religion and astute with the learned people of the day, so much so that You stayed in the temple in Jerusalem when Your parents thought You were playing with the other children. You respected Your Jewish culture and began Your earthly ministry at the appropriate age of thirty. You were baptized in the river Jordan by Your cousin and forerunner, John the Baptist. You were tempted by Satan and overcame triumphantly.

You preached in parables and held people's attention for hours. You healed the sick, raised the dead, delivered maniacs, changed water to wine, opened blind eyes and deaf ears. You cursed the unproductive fig tree and paid taxes with a coin from the mouth of a fish. You praised the gift of the poor widow's pennies and drove the money changers out of the temple.

You had twelve best friends. Ten of them didn't really know You. One of them betrayed You and another denied You, even though both looked to You to save them when trouble came.

You were called a son of Satan, a blasphemer. You were run out of Your own hometown. You rode into Jerusalem with a crowd of revelers one week, and the very next week they exchanged You for a criminal named Barabbas and cried, "Crucify Him! Crucify Him!" You were mocked, scorned, drugged, beaten, cursed, spit on, lied about, gambled over, laughed at, nailed to a cross, stabbed in the side, given vinegar for Your parched throat. You could have leaped down off that cross and slaughtered every man and woman there, but instead You hung for six hours while onlookers waited for You to die.

While You were hanging there, You proved what You said, "I have overcome the world." You answered the cry of the thief being crucified next to You when he pleaded, "Lord, remember me when You come into Your kingdom." You gave him *good cheer*. You assured him, "Today you will be with Me in Paradise" (Luke 23:42–43 NKJV).

If Your life had stopped there, Jesus, we would be convinced that You thoroughly and unequivocally experienced every possible thing that we human beings can experience in our lives. That alone is such a comfort. But, hallelujah, the story does not end at Your death! Three days later You triumphed over all tribulation and evil by rising from Your tomb with all power in heaven and earth in Your hands. Supernatural power to conquer and overcome everything that we encounter in both the natural world and the spiritual realm.

Nearly eight hundred years before You were born, the prophet Isaiah told us You were coming. He proclaimed, "For unto us a child is born, unto us a son is given: and the government shall be upon his shoulder: and his name shall be called Wonderful, Counselor, The mighty God, The everlasting Father, The Prince of Peace. Of the increase of his government and peace there shall be no end" (Isa. 9:6–7 KJV).

When You ascended to the Father, we entered the dispensation of grace and favor. You said in Luke 4:18–19 (NIV),

> The Spirit of the Lord is on me,
>   because he has anointed me
>   to preach good news to the poor.
> He has sent me to proclaim freedom for the prisoners
>   and recovery of sight for the blind,
> to release the oppressed,
>   to proclaim the year of the Lord's favor.

You came to earth, bled and died, and rose again as our never-failing Messiah who has helped and will help us in every—and I mean *every*—situation to triumph in tribulation.

Dear reader, dear friend, just as Jesus conquered death and has all power in heaven and earth in His hands, He will use His power to give *you* authority to triumph over any problem you are facing. Girl, you are not just a survivor; you are more than a conqueror through Christ Jesus!

I call you friend because I hope you will take what we talk about as coming from someone who cares about you. Friends are comforters, confidants, and confronters who are committed to helping you deal effectively with every situation. Friends care about your well-being. Friends love you for who you are—and in spite of who you are. Friends will stand up for you when you're right and gently tell you when you're wrong. The Bible says that a friend sticks closer to you than a brother (or sister!). Please consider me your friend.

As your friend, I will probably call you affectionate names such as Sweetie, Baby, and Honey. Indulge me. I'm from the South. It's just the way I talk. I will more than likely get pretty specific about some things that may make you uncomfortable. Please don't stop reading. There will be lots of good news in what I have to say.

There may be a group of ladies that you'd like to have over for coffee so you can discuss some of these topics together. I love interacting with groups of people. There's such a wonderful exchange of wisdom and experience, so much healing. I have a circle of friends who get together to have fun. Often, we end up spending our fun time discussing issues, going to the Scriptures to find the answers to our questions, and having a good ol' prayer meeting where we submit our concerns to the only One who has all the answers.

Sister and friend, thank you for inviting me into your life today. We will enjoy our conversations together. Let the tears you may shed and the laughter I hope you'll experience wash over your soul and bring you healing and wholeness. Remember, Girl, *nothing* happens to you that God doesn't already have the answer to. If that isn't good news, I don't know what is!

BEE encouraged,

Thelma

1

I'm Fighting Depression

Thelma, I feel like I'm losing my mind. I want out of here. Out of this life. It's too hard. People are too cruel. Nothing goes right. My life is a mess, and I just can't take it anymore. I can't seem to think straight. I want to scream. I feel like I'm going to jump out of my skin. Nothing brings me any pleasure. I can't stop crying. I don't even know what I'm crying about.

My friends avoid me. The ladies at church plan things but never invite me. My mother came to stay with me for a while, but we couldn't get along. I had a man friend for a while, but lately he has stopped calling or dropping by. Oh, well, that's the story of my life. Nobody appreciates me. I can't please anybody. Everybody leaves. It seems the better I try to be to people, the worse they treat me. It's not worth it. I just don't see the point of life anymore.

I tried to talk to a friend at work about how I'm feeling, and she wants me to go to some clinic and talk to a counselor. I refuse to go, and I definitely won't take any medicine. I've seen counselors before, and they're all as crazy as I am. Most of them need to be sitting on their own couches working through their own problems. I'm not going to spill my guts to some stranger who just wants my money.

I don't know what to do, Thelma. I have to force myself to go through the motions every day because all I really want to do is sleep. Maybe one day I'll just sleep on out of here. Who would care? Nobody!

Thelma, I don't know if you're listening to me, either. You probably think I'm crazy too.

❧

Listen to me, Baby, and listen good: you are definitely not crazy. Thousands of other women have felt the way you do right now. I've been one of them. I don't know of a person alive who has not, at one time or another, experienced bouts with depression. Sometimes it's a natural result of temporary circumstances; it lasts a few hours or days, and it's simply unavoidable in this world. Other times it parks, settling in for a long visit.

My experience with serious depression lasted nearly a year. I had crying spells like you're describing, shouting matches with loved ones and strangers, even fainting spells. (I found out later they were not really fainting spells because I could remember everything going on around me when I'd zone out.) But my emotional states of fantasy and confusion got more and more frequent as the year progressed.

Finally, my doctor put me in the hospital, ran some tests to see what was causing the "fainting," and discovered by talking with me that my biggest problem was feeling trapped in my marriage, trapped with two babies in diapers, trapped by an ailing great-grandmother I was responsible to care for. I was afraid of losing my husband because my appearance had changed. He had started a new company, and I didn't see him as much as I wanted to. I was scared that my beloved granny was going to die. I was convinced that none of my friends liked me anymore. I hated staying at home doing all the housework and meeting my motherly, wifely responsibilities. I was a mess! All of which caused me to focus on myself and my predicament rather than on the good things around me that were mine to relish every day. Angry, disappointed with life, disillusioned because my dreams were not living up to my expectations, I plummeted into depression.

My doctor was great. He called a spade a spade. After finding out how I really felt about my life, my marriage, my children, my whole situation, he saw straight through the fog in my mind and told me to get involved in something bigger than myself. "Get out of the house more, Thelma! Get a job. Volunteer. Stop seeing yourself as a victim. Victims never win! Your problem is that your lifestyle changed so rapidly that you have not caught up with it. Go back to doing some of the things you did before the children came along. Realize that depression usually masks anger. Find out what you're mad about, and deal with it in a constructive way."

This remedy worked for me, and it might be part of the solution for you, too, if you're willing to try it. You seem to be angry and disappointed at life as I was, full of fear and sure that you're all alone. Baby, listen to me. As far as somebody caring whether you sleep away from here or not, the fact is, *I care*. And whether you believe it or not, your family and friends care. Taking yourself out would get attention, but not the kind you deserve. You deserve a full, healthy, good life. Don't give up before you get it!

❧

Change the way you talk to yourself. Girl, do you talk to yourself? Do you ask yourself questions? Do you answer those questions? Do you interrupt yourself before you get an answer? If you do, you're in good company. Some of the best decisions you can make are between you and yourself. Most people who talk to themselves are not crazy; they're at least talking to someone intelligent for a change. So, it's fine to talk to yourself if you're saying the right things.

The wrong way to talk to yourself is to talk down to yourself. Refrain from saying things like, "I can't do anything right." "What's wrong with me?" "I am so stupid." "I can't get anywhere on time." "Things just don't work out right for me." "I'm sick and tired of being sick and tired." "They don't like me." "I'm such a loser." "People are always jerking me around." "I hate this." "Trouble just seems to find me." "I don't care what happens." "Life is hard and then you die."

Do not say these negative things to yourself. No! No! No! What you put into your mind will settle in your spirit and come out of your mouth. Don't even think about it, Girl. Change the way you talk to *you*.

I believe in affirmations. An affirmation is a positive statement spoken in first-person singular, present tense, as if it had already happened. Here are some affirmations. Repeat them after me:

"I like myself."

"Things work out well for me."

"I am attractive and charming."

"I enjoy life."

"I am blessed."

"I am healthy."

"I am appreciated."

"I enjoy rest and relaxation."

"I like people."

"I am successful."

"I am progressing in my career."

"I love my family."

"I have wonderful friends."

"I cherish the gift of life."

"I have all the money I need to do whatever I want."

Now, stop laughing. If you keep saying it and working toward it, you'll make room in your life for God to make it all come true.

Baby, it is so important to speak to yourself positively. I read somewhere that your body will follow where your mind leads. What I mean by all this is, when you change your focus from the negatives about you to the positives about you, you refocus your attention away from what's bringing you down to what can bring you up.

❧

Get it all out. Each of us has problems that need talking out. You've already started the healing process because you're willing to talk to me about how you feel. Now you need to find someone who is available to you, someone who can be objective and keep your confidence and talk out everything you feel with her. I know you're a private person and don't want to tell people your feelings, but you've got to get rid of all the pain you're carrying around inside.

Be careful whom you choose to confide in. When we're feeling low and bad about ourselves, we tend to gravitate toward people who will treat us just as we think we deserve: bad. Affirm within yourself that you deserve to have a safe, wise, loving person to talk to, and then seek out that person. Reach out for help. Be open to that person's insights and suggestions. Look for solutions; don't just focus on where you're stuck.

Another great way to get out all your feelings in a safe way is to write them out. In writing, you can express things you would never say to a person directly. I suggest that you find a notebook and a pen. Sit down and write a letter to the person or persons you're angry with. Say everything in the letter that comes to your mind even if it's vulgar, mean, stupid, insulting, or surprising to you. Get it down on paper. *Do not mail the letter!*

Next, write the person or persons a second letter, telling them in no uncertain terms everything you failed to tell them in the first letter. *Again, do not mail the letter!*

Finally, write a third letter. By this time, you should have gotten a lot of hurt out of your system. Continue writing until you feel relieved that you have told them everything you need or want to.

At some point you may be able to have a rational, healing conversation with the person who has hurt you, but sometimes that's not possible or even necessary. The important thing is to dump the pain and stop focusing on it. When you think about bad things all the time, you're going to feel bad!

Honey, I hope you're beginning to recognize how unresolved anger is playing a part in your depression. It's crucial for you to get that angry poison out of your system in a way that won't hurt you or others. Once you get it out, the healing can go faster.

⚜

Take care of your physical health. How is your appetite? Are you eating fruits, vegetables, and grains? Are you eating three balanced meals a day? Are you drinking the amount of water you need? These questions may seem strange, but your physical body needs attention when you feel down in the dumps like you do.

When we get depressed, we usually don't eat correctly, we eat too much, or we don't eat at all. If this is true of you, then get some nutritious food so you can feel better and think clearer.

Also, do some kind of exercise every day. Stretch, walk, jog, ride a bike, swim, do something to get your body functioning properly. Eating right and exercising alone can start you on your way to a healthier physical and emotional life. Sure, you'll have to force yourself to do these things. The hardest part is getting started. Stop reading right now and get up and eat and do five minutes of some kind of exercise.

Do it now!

Welcome back. Now, I know you said you won't take any medicine, but do you want to get well or not? I'm not going to try to talk you into spilling your guts to a counselor week after week, but I'd be doing you a disservice if I didn't urge you to get a psychiatric evaluation. Don't freak out on me here; I'm not saying you're a nut case. But you need to be aware that many people who suffer from depression have a very real chemical imbalance in the brain, and they need medical treatment to get back their equilibrium. Baby, I urge you to make an appointment with a psychiatrist—a medical doctor who is trained in neurochemistry and can properly evaluate your physical and mental condition.

If it turns out that you can benefit from one of the safe, modern antidepressants available, then please be open! How long and hard you suffer is partly your choice. Get all the help you possibly can, Honey, 'cause life is short. Don't spend one minute longer than you need to feeling bad about yourself and your life.

❧

Get outside yourself. Granny used to say, "Child, an idle mind is the devil's workshop." That is soooo true. When you have a lot of time on your hands to think, you'll think of the wrong thing. So stay busy. Choose to focus on things larger than yourself.

Doing something for others who cannot do for themselves—and expecting nothing in return—is one of the best ways I know to get outside oneself. Volunteer with a nonprofit organization that helps feed the hungry and care for the poor. Tutor children at schools or teach people to read. Visit hospitals and nursing homes, combing people's hair or listening to their stories. Ask your friends about themselves rather than talking only about your problems. Become involved with your church. And remember when you do that, other people have problems just like you do. Don't expect them to be any more perfect than you are.

The best way to get outside yourself is to keep looking up to God, the Author and Finisher of your faith. God cares about you when nobody else does. He is the only Person who will be with you every second of every minute of every hour of every day for the rest of your life. He is as close as the air you breathe. Nothing escapes Him. He is the only Person who completely knows how you feel and why you feel that way. Ask God to help you through His Son, Jesus.

Psalm 121:1–2 (KJV) is such a powerful proclamation: "I will lift up mine eyes unto the hills, from whence cometh my help. My help cometh from the LORD, which made heaven and earth." Read and digest that entire psalm, my friend. Every time you start to get down in the dumps, meditate on these words:

He will not suffer thy foot to be moved: he that keepeth thee will not slumber. Behold, he that keepeth Israel shall neither slumber nor sleep. (Ps. 121:3–4 KJV)

Start right now, Baby. Get your Bible and read this. Proclaim out loud, "My help comes from the Lord!" Or just say, "HELP ME, JESUS!" He will. He's always just a prayer away.

———————— ✦ ————————

Dear Jesus, *we thank You for being available twenty-four hours a day to help us when we're in distress. When we get down, You promise to lift us up. When we're lonely, we trust You to be our Friend. When we have nobody to talk to but ourselves, we know You will listen. Loving Lord, assure my dear sister that You are closer than her own breath, that You care and will help whenever she calls on You. Give her the courage to face all her feelings of anger and fear head-on, and to trust You to take her depression and send it far, far away where it can no longer steal her joy of living. Thank You, Jesus, for helping her right now. In Your powerful name we pray, amen.*

2

I'm Suffering from Abuse

Thelma, I can identify with you when you talk about being put in a closet when you were a child. When I was a little girl, I was put in the cellar of our house. Sometimes I was locked in the bathroom for hours.

One of my relatives sexually abused me from the time I was eight years old. My mother never acknowledged that she knew it. I would try to tell her, and she would shrug it off as if I was making it all up. I hated him for doing it and hated my mother for allowing it. Now every time I see either one of them, my blood boils. I've tried to have a decent relationship with my mother, but I can't. She's so hoity-toity at church. Everybody thinks she's never done anything wrong. She makes me sick to my stomach.

It's really weird. I hate my mother and love her at the same time. The same is true for the person who abused me. It's a constant struggle to keep my wits and not go off on them. I can see why people commit murder. I've even thought about it. I'm ashamed to admit that the main reason I haven't is that I'm afraid of going to prison and being molested there.

When I was little, I constantly felt ashamed, violated, dirty, frustrated, agitated, and worthless. Now that I'm grown, not much has changed inside or out. I seem to gravitate to people just like the ones I always wanted to get away from.

I've been married to my second husband for three years. My first one was just plain mean, almost from the beginning. Since I was only eighteen when we got married, and he started hitting me the second month, I just moved home to get away from him for a while. He told me if I didn't like being his wife, then I could just find myself someone else. He said I'd never find anyone else who'd put up with me. I knew he was probably right, but I divorced him anyway. I figured if I was going to feel bad, I might as well do it at home where there was no one beating me up.

My husband now has always been a charmer. He treats me real good, makes me feel like a princess. But then, out of nowhere, he gets furious with me. Tells me that I'm a no-good blankety-blank and that I look like something the cat dragged in. I never know what sets him off. A couple of weeks ago when I disagreed with him about something so minor I can't even remember what it was, he grabbed my arm so hard he left bruises. One of my friends told me to call the police next time he tries to lay a hand on me so the authorities will have a record of his abuse. I don't want to do that. I don't want my husband in jail or labeled an abuser. I don't want to be alone.

Every relationship I've ever had has been abusive and confusing.

I can't seem to break the cycle. Maybe I deserve it. Maybe God's punishing me for something. Maybe I was born to be abused.

❧

Honey, let me set you straight on one thing right this minute: *You were not born to be abused!* Nobody was born to be abused. God's loving concern for you and the value He places on every human being are in sharp contrast to abuse. When God created you, He intended for you to be safe and protected, not battered and bruised. In every incident of abuse—whether subtle or overt—moral, ethical, and spiritual laws are being violated. God's plan for you is being perverted because He never intended for you to be mistreated. He loves you too much. You are precious in His sight.

Jesus gave His life for you so that you would know to the core of your being that He does not want you to suffer abuse like He did on your behalf. The Holy Spirit lives in you, guiding you into the truth that He came to comfort you. When you are abused, God is grieved, Jesus pleads your case for you, and the Holy Spirit wants to guide you through and out of that situation.

Get this straight, Sweetheart: You were not born to be abused. You were born to be loved.

❧

Jesus loves you. If you have received Him as your personal Savior, then you are God's beloved child, bought with the highest price that's ever been paid. I asked Jesus to live in my heart when I was only four years old, so when my mother's mother locked me in the closet, I felt Jesus' presence even in the midst of my grandmother's abuse. God would remind me of Christian hymns and choruses I'd learned, and I spent a lot of my "closet time" singing.

One of the songs I sang that is just as true for you now as it was for me then is this:

> Jesus loves me!
> This I know, for the Bible tells me so.
> Little ones to Him belong;
> They are weak, but He is strong.
> Yes, Jesus loves me!
> Yes, Jesus loves me!
> Yes, Jesus loves me!
> The Bible tells me so.

Jesus longs to comfort you, Baby, and to let you feel His loving care.

I can imagine that throughout your life, even in the darkest times, you must have felt Someone protecting the deepest part of you. I just don't believe you could have made it this far without that protection. Think about it. Someone kept you alive physically and spiritually and is giving you the strength to talk about your situation. Someone is letting you know that it's time to do something about it.

Don't be a victim. Any kind of abuse can leave your soul purposeless, your spirit drained, your body sick. You take and take and take it until you are convinced that this is your lot in life. But being abused wasn't God's will for you as a child, and it certainly isn't His plan for you as an adult! When you were little, you did not ask to be abused, did not deserve to be abused, and could not control being abused. It happened to you just as it happens to thousands of children in this sin-darkened world. But as a woman of God, you can choose a different path. Girl, give up the victim mentality because victims never win!

The truth is, nobody can tell you how much abuse to take. But don't fool yourself into believing that God is pleased about your staying in abusive relationships. God did not call you to be a martyr for no cause. Remember, there are plenty of women who have ended up dead as a result of staying with abusive partners. Even if your life isn't in danger right this minute, your soul is.

Sweetie, I'm proud of you for already beginning the healing process. You are talking to somebody about it. I suggest that you seek godly counsel through a church, clinic, or Christian therapist. These people face this issue every day, and they have the expertise to help you. Determine to change your life for the better. There are excellent books on abuse survival in the library.

Find out how other people have changed, and ask God for the courage to follow in their footsteps. Act like the redeemed, beloved-by-God woman that you are!

❦

Ask God for direction. I cannot tell you specifically what to do to heal your relationships, let go of your bitterness, or get out of danger. However, God can and will give you clarity about what to do. Matthew 7:7–8 (NKJV) tells you to "ask, and it will be given to you; seek, and you will find; knock, and it will be opened to you. For everyone who asks receives, and he who seeks finds, and to him who knocks it will be opened."

Honey, you can have full assurance that God will give you direction for handling your abusive situation. God is as close as your thoughts. In your mind as well as with your mouth, you can ask God to show you the way, and He will. You can ask God to heal your hurts. You can ask Him to restore your self-confidence. You can ask Him to help you forgive your abusers and your mother while keeping yourself safe from their further violations. You can ask Him to give you joy, peace, and contentment. You can ask Him to remove you from your harmful situation and to give you courage to make healthy choices. You can even ask Him to change the person(s) abusing you.

Practically speaking, be determined to change your life. Wait on God, but don't be foolishly passive. I encourage you to contact the authorities about the physical abuse you've experienced. Find refuge away from your husband in a place where you can be protected and truly supported. Don't let your husband manipulate you into coming back unless he has gotten help, and it has proven successful.

❧

Keep the faith. As you seek God's guidance in faith, He will place in your mind a place, person, process, system, or something that will help you in your particular situation. He is concerned about you because He made you in His image and wants you to have the very best that life can give.

Sometimes when you ask Him for help, you won't see Him working with your natural eye. Don't worry. He *promises* to work in *all* things for your good (Rom. 8:28). So thank Him daily for what He's doing in your life. Listen carefully for His voice. And commit yourself to following His directions.

I have discovered that when He tells us what to do, there is always peace in the spirit. When He's not the One directing us, there is usually confusion or an uneasy feeling. I call it a gut feeling. Follow your gut, Baby, and you probably won't go wrong. When you don't know what to do, don't do anything. Wait patiently. Jesus will come through for you.

Sweetheart, you are not in this alone. You have my prayerful support, the love of family and friends, and most of all, Jesus

Christ Himself pleading your case at the right hand of His Father, the Lord God almighty.

Father, *You know all about my sister who has been wounded in the past and is being wounded now. You know the plans You have for her. Help her to know that those plans do not include abuse in her life. Please, Lord, let her know deep within her mind and heart that You are the Source of her escape. Speak to her clearly, and tell her what steps to take to correct her situation. At the same time, Lord, give her a heart of forgiveness for the people who have so cruelly harmed her. Draw this family together with love so that the rest of their days can be happy together. It is Your will for everybody to be healthy. So, Father, we ask for deliverance and healing for the abusers in this sister's life. Especially let her husband know You and Your grace and mercy. Do not render to him justice unless his heart is so hardened that You know he will never change. We trust You, Father, to keep Your word of comfort and protection in times of trouble. Thank You for hearing our prayer. In the name of Jesus, amen.*

3

I've Had an Abortion

Thelma, sometimes I can hardly stand it. I wake up in the morning thinking about it. I go to work thinking about it. I can't sleep sometimes, thinking about it. It consumes my life.

I wonder if my baby was a boy or girl. I wonder what it would have looked like; how it would have done in school; if it would have played sports or been a ballerina or a singer. I wonder if it really is in heaven and if I'll recognize it in the hereafter.

I imagine playing on the beach, getting wet and covered with sand as we create sand castles. I can see us going to the library and doing homework together; stopping to get a hot dog and having mustard and relish whooshing out of the corners of our mouths. I wonder what color graduation gown my baby would have worn for kindergarten, high school, and college. What kind of person would my baby have married? How many grandchildren would I have had?

Oh, Thelma, it's torment! I will never get over what I've done. I am so angry with myself. How can I ever forgive myself for doing that? How can God ever forgive me for doing that? That was the worst mistake of my life. I feel horrible!

I really wanted my baby, but I was afraid of what people might say. I was also worried about how people would treat my baby without a father. I had so many fears. I was just a child. I thought I was doing what was right, the best thing to do at the time.

I know other people who have had abortions, and it doesn't seem to bother them one bit. They even talk about it to me. I try to pretend that it's not bothering me, but it's tearing me up. They don't even know I've had an abortion. I'm too ashamed to tell them. There are only three people in the world who know. Now, you're the fourth.

Thelma, I cannot continue living like this. I need some relief. I need some help.

❧

Honey, there was a time in my life when I might have made the same decision you did. I was under the impression that it was all right to have an abortion in the first trimester because I had seen some of my friends have one and it seemed harmless. I thought it was just a blood clot and no baby had formed, so what was the harm? God revealed the truth to me some years later. Fortunately for me, I didn't have to make that decision.

When we make those kinds of decisions, we think they are right at the time. We don't know what else to do. We are usually thinking about the immediate circumstances, not the consequences. Our feelings are as natural as breathing. We think, *I've got to do something about this. This can't be happening to me. I've got to take care of this problem.* So, to protect ourselves and our loved ones, we make choices.

Possibly, nobody told us of the fallout of the decision. We get these feelings of remorse, anger, guilt, shame, horror, and more. Actually, they are the same feelings we get when we commit any well-thought-out sin.

Baby, I understand some of what you're dealing with. Even though I've not had to deal with the aftermath of an abortion, I have sinned and come short of the glory of God.

❧

Sin is sin. One of the great things about God is that He doesn't categorize sin. Sin is sin. No little sins, no big sins, just Sin with a capital *S*. All sin separates us from God if we don't have salvation through Christ Jesus.

The other marvelous thing about God is that He forgives sin and doesn't remember it anymore. No, there's nothing wrong with God's memory—but He chooses never to remind us of what we've confessed. When we are reminded and feel hurt again, the enemy, Satan, wants us to feel bad.

I've been a victim of Satan's target practice more than once. You see, I'm a child of lust, not love. My mother and father were not married. Society has tried to label me "illegitimate," and the enemy has tried to make me feel less valuable than people who come from "good" parents. No! I refuse to accept a negative label. My parents might have had an illegitimate relationship, but I'm not illegitimate. I did nothing to get here.

Thank God, my mother valued life enough to allow me to be born or didn't have a choice in the matter. Whatever! I'm just glad I'm here. However, it's gratifying to know that even if she'd decided to abort me, God would have forgiven her if she'd asked. I possibly would be in heaven waiting for her to come, so we would live together forever in a perfect world, in heaven, where there is no sorrow, hurt, illegitimacy, stigma, or any bad thing.

❦

God can make you whole again. Those feelings of embarrassment, guilt, shame, remorse, condemnation, bitterness, frustration, anger, torment, and depression about what you've done may weigh you down. But, Girl, have I got good news for you: *there is no sin so bad that God will not forgive it.* In fact, Sweetie, a huge part of His nature is forgiveness.

When you repent (really meaning what you say), He hears you and forgives you and washes you as white as snow. He separates your sin from you as far as the East is from the West, and you know East will never touch West. Just listen to this:

> Blessed are they
> > whose transgressions are forgiven,
> > whose sins are covered.

Blessed is the man
>> whose sin the Lord will never count against him.

> (Rom. 4:7–8 NIV)

Hallelujah!

I don't know of a person who has avoided making an unwise, uninformed, unscrupulous decision. Sure, some of those decisions cannot be undone; we must live with them. There are consequences to everything we do or say. But through His Son, Jesus, God has made a way so that we can be forgiven, restored, and made whole again. God promises,

> Though your sins are like scarlet,
>> they shall be as white as snow;
> though they are red as crimson,
>> they shall be like wool.

> (Isa. 1:18 NIV)

Girl, is that good news or what?

❧

Give it up to God. If I were you, Baby, the first thing I'd do is tell God how much you hurt and how sorry you are. I'd believe in my heart that He's listening and doing something about it. Be willing to give all your pain and guilt to God. Stop beating yourself up. Be willing to forgive yourself by accepting His forgiveness. Ask God for the *desire* to unburden yourself once and for all, then turn it over to Him.

As you're talking to God, tell Him that you want all the debilitating emotions of what has happened to be taken from you. Allow the Holy Spirit to reveal to you every emotion you feel. Ask Jesus to take them one at a time.

For example: *your feelings of remorse.* Tell Jesus you don't want these feelings of remorse anymore. Give them to Him to take away, so you will never feel them again. Tell Jesus you lay these feelings at His feet for Him to destroy. Tell Satan that he cannot torment you anymore with feelings of remorse, that the demon of remorse must bow at the feet of Jesus; you *will not* tolerate that any longer. Ask Jesus to fill that place of remorse with gladness, which you receive from the riches that are yours in Christ Jesus. Repeat this exercise with each individual emotion until you don't feel it anymore.

I know this exercise works because I have done it myself and have been in the presence of other people who have done it. Sometimes it takes hours and days to go through this process because it takes time for you to give up how you feel. You've been feeling it for a long time, and it may actually feel awkward to let go of your burden. But I know from experience that the instant you really give it up, God takes it away. He sets you free. And anyone the Son sets free is free indeed!

If you don't feel comfortable with this process, you might consider writing down everything you feel about the situation. I mean *everything*. It doesn't matter how bad you think it is or how you verbalize it to God. He will not fall off His throne. Just get it down on paper. After you finish writing, hold the paper up in your hands, and offer it to God for Him to take. Just say, "Here's my mess, God. Please take it. Please forgive me, and release me from the bondage of thoughts, feelings, imaginations, and despair. I surrender this to You. Help me forgive myself, and make me whole again. In Jesus' name, amen."

The next thing I'd do is talk to my baby and tell it I'm sorry. That may sound silly, but I think it would help you. Perhaps you could write your little unborn one a letter, pouring out all your thoughts, regrets, dreams, blessings, and love. Your child is safe in the arms of Jesus, Baby. You're the one who needs release. Tell your baby how much you love it, and then let Jesus take care of it for eternity.

❧

Cling to God's love for you. Trust God that God is doing for you what He has done for zillions of people throughout the world for generations. He loves you with an everlasting love. Your decision did not and does not stop God from loving you. Just as you love your child whom you have not seen, *God loves you even more.* You have not seen God, but He sees and watches over you every day, all day. Not one hair grows on your head that He does not know and care about. That's why you can ask Him to replenish those empty places that the debilitating emotions carved out of you with the ability to love, praise, be thankful, laugh again—and even think about your baby with feelings of joy.

I know all of this sounds unreal right now. But you brought your burden to me, and I'm telling you stuff that works. Don't ask me how it works. It's a mystery to me too. I just know it does because I've experienced it many times before. Throughout the country at the conferences where I speak, women tell me that they thought I was really off the wall when I told them to do that, but they thought it wouldn't hurt to try. Now they attest to the fact that it works!

Reflect on 1 John 1:8–9 (NKJV): "If we say that we have no sin, we deceive ourselves, and the truth is not in us. If we confess our sins, He is faithful and just to forgive us our sins and to cleanse us from all unrighteousness." Commit this scripture to memory. Every time you feel those painful emotions trying to come back, recite this passage. Say it again and again until it becomes a part of you, especially the part that starts with, "If we confess our sins . . ." Change the wording to first person: "If I confess my sins, He is faithful and just to forgive me and to cleanse me from all unrighteousness." That's *all* unrighteousness, Honey. Not just about the decisions you made when you had an abortion, but every decision you've made and will ever make to sin.

Remember, God has set you free from the bondage of sin. When God forgives and sets free, He never washes your face with it again. It's over. Case closed. A big ten-four. Now, are you going to give God a chance to forgive you and take away those awful feelings? He's waiting. He wants to set you free!

Father, *thank You for allowing us to come to You boldly and tell You* everything. *This precious child of Yours needs Your forgiveness and Your assurance. She needs You to take all of her negative, debilitating emotions about her abortion and make her clean again. Lord, I've seen You do it again and again. I know You'll do it for her. Please speak peace to her spirit. As You break this yoke of bondage that has plagued her for so long, create a coat of personal forgiveness, mercy, grace, peace, contentment, and continual blessing for her. Let her know that You love her, and there's nothing she can do about that! Let her know You've never left her, that in her darkest hour You were there. Give her the assurance that she is released from the guilt, shame, remorse, bitterness, and destruction her decisions caused. Assure her that You have wiped her slate clean and she is whiter than snow. In Jesus' righteous name we pray, amen.*

4

I'm Plagued by Worry and Fear

Thelma, I've heard Christians talk about having a peace they can't explain, but I don't have that peace. There are times when I think I have peace, but then something will come up to unnerve me. Instantly, it becomes obvious that I don't have the kind of peace I keep hearing about.

I thought I would have peace when I married my husband. He's a good husband, a loving father, and a great provider. He tries to give me everything I want. It's embarrassing for me to say this, but the more he gives, the more I want. I never feel really safe. I actually have everything I need and almost everything I want, but it's not enough to make me feel secure.

Maybe I don't understand what peace really is. My friends make statements like these: "I just need a little peace." "Lord, give me peace." "What the world needs is peace." "Pray for peace." I believe they are asking for different kinds of peace. Peace in world affairs. Peaceful rest and relaxation. Peaceful relationships. That's not what

I mean when I long for peace. I want to feel something in my soul that assures me that everything is going to be all right. I have a lot of anxiety. Yes, my life is great right now, but what if the bottom dropped out of my world?

I go to church, but usually, I leave as empty as I went. I can't even find rest from my worries in church. I wonder if other people have as many fears as I do. I've read in your books about how God gave you peace when your granddaughter was sick. Your great-grandmother had a stroke, and God gave your little girl peace to believe Granny was going to recover. God even gave you peace when your grandmother locked you in a closet! I'm afraid that kind of peace will always remain just a pipe dream for me.

Thelma, I know that suddenly, without warning, storms can come. What will I do when they come? I've never had a bad storm, just some scattered rain showers. It frightens me to think that one day I'll have to go through really tough times. I get so scared when I think about it!

Where can I get peace, Thelma? How can I stop worrying? I'm tired of being afraid all the time.

Sweetie, I think you have just expressed the sentiment of everybody in the world. God's intent for humankind was to live peacefully in a world of peace. But the peace God gave to His creation was disrupted by the disobedience of the first man and woman, Adam and Eve. As a result, our peace can be disrupted often by negative thoughts, bad news, frightening medical reports, lack of financial stability, wayward children, unfaithful spouses, conditional love, quarrels and fights, crime, wars and rumors of wars, changes in circumstances—the list can go on and into next week.

There is no way to avoid some of life's scary situations. God does not guarantee us that storms will go around us. Rather, He promises to be in control of every storm. Understanding that with your heart, not just your head, makes the difference.

Peace is a direct by-product of faith in Christ. A lot of people look for peace in all the wrong places, don't they? Some look for relief from worry and fear in alcohol, drugs, food, gambling, sexual promiscuity, a mate, a position, status, prestige, money, possessions, fame, glamour, religion, preachers and pastors, education, power, family members, friends, planning and plotting, wishful thinking, aimless day-dreaming, sports and physical activities, travel, exploration and adventure, science, sabbaticals, and more. But Scripture teaches us that peace and other spiritual blessings are a direct result of faith in Christ. Yes, the destruction of peace was the result of the fall of humanity; but praise God, He made a way for each of us to regain peace in the midst of tribulation!

Because Satan initiated the destruction of peace in the world, the destruction of Satan must occur in order to reestablish peace. Well, guess what, Sweetie? God sent Jesus to destroy the devil and to reconcile people to the Father so we can have a peace that passes understanding! Jesus' death and resurrection disarmed and conquered the hostile forces of Satan and his agents and made peace possible. When we truly believe in Jesus Christ and receive Him in our hearts as Lord of our lives, He justifies us through our faith and assures us peace with God. The only true peace comes from a relationship with Him.

Once you have accepted Christ and received Him in your heart, the Spirit of peace comes to live within you in the person of the Holy Spirit: "The fruit of the Spirit is love, joy, *peace*, patience, kindness, goodness, faithfulness, gentleness and self-control" (Gal. 5:22–23 NIV, emphasis is added). This spiritual fruit is available to all Christians at the moment of salvation.

If you have been born again into God's family and still find yourself plagued by worry and fear, then you need to pray that God will increase your awareness of the Spirit who lives within you. Through faith in Christ, you have everything it takes right inside your spirit to live in peace. Pray that God will activate His spiritual fruit in your daily life. Jesus promised, "The Counselor, the Holy Spirit, whom the Father will send in my name, will teach you all things and will remind you of everything I have said to you. Peace I leave with you; my peace I give you. I do not give to you as the world gives. Do not let your hearts be troubled and do not be afraid" (John 14:26–27 NIV).

❧

Live in the present. Darlin', it's pretty clear that a lot of your worries are about what-if's. *What if something bad happens? How will I cope if a storm comes? If my world falls apart, will I?* Oh, what a vicious cycle that kind of worry and projection is!

Jesus understood so well that our minds work that way. That's why He gave us this instruction in His Sermon on the Mount: "Therefore I tell you, do not worry about your life, what you will eat or drink; or about your body, what you will wear . . . Do not worry about tomorrow, for tomorrow will worry about itself. Each day has enough trouble of its own" (Matt. 6:25, 34 NIV).

Honey, if you keep telling yourself scary stories about all the scary things that might happen, you're going to get scared! Stop it! Take your thoughts captive in obedience to Christ, and choose to focus on how He's providing for you right here and now. God will keep in perfect peace the person whose mind is stayed on *Him* (Isa. 26:3). Even if things aren't so purty for you in the present, He's still here, making sure that you have what you need to be okay. Paul assured us of that truth: "My God will meet all your needs according to his glorious riches in Christ Jesus" (Phil. 4:19 NIV). Girl, that means *all*.

I love to sing this hymn:

> When peace, like a river, attendeth my way,
> When sorrow, like sea billows roll;
> Whatever my lot,

> Thou hast taught me to say,
> It is well,
> It is well with my soul.

When I was locked in the closet as a little girl, I sang the great hymns of my faith. Try singing the glorious truths of God, Baby. Make them your own. Be determined to replace your scary stories with the glorious Story of Faith.

❧

Meditate on God's promises. A few years ago in the month of January, I was praying for God to give me a scripture that would sustain me in the coming months. When I got off my knees, I turned on Christian television, and there was a man saying, "Some of you want to know a scripture that will help you during this year. Turn in your Bibles to Philippians 4, and read with me."

I hurriedly opened my Bible to Philippians and started reading along with the preacher. When we got to the sixth verse, I knew that God wanted me to read, chew on, swallow, and digest these words for that year: "Be anxious for nothing. But in all things with prayer and supplication, with thanksgiving, let your petition be made known to God, and the God of peace which surpasses understanding will guard your heart and your mind, through Christ Jesus."

Little did I know that the year was going to start and finish with me having to remind myself of that scripture more times than I wanted be reminded! That was a tough year for me. If I had not meditated constantly on that specific scripture, I don't think I would have made it. But I did what the verse said: I took petition after petition straight to God, and with a thankful heart that didn't leave room for anxiety, I left all my requests with Him. And you know what? He took care of them. Not always in the exact way I wanted, but in the exact way I needed.

When God promises peace, Sister, He means peace! Take Him at His *Word!*

> You are a shield around me, O LORD;
> you bestow glory on me and lift up my head.
> To the LORD I cry aloud,
> and he answers me from his holy hill.
> I lie down and sleep;
> I wake again, because the LORD sustains me.
> I will not fear the tens of thousands
> drawn up against me on every side . . .
> From the LORD comes deliverance.
> May your blessing be on your people.
> (Ps. 3:3–6, 8 NIV)

The only real peace comes from taking God at His Word, enfleshed in Christ Jesus. If you have truly made Jesus the Lord of your life and trust Him for everything, He will give you indescribable peace in *all* your circumstances.

———————————— ✑ ————————————

Dear Lord Jesus, *Thank You that through Your Spirit living within us, we can have peace in this life in spite of circumstances. Your perfect peace surrounds us every day as we go about our routines. When we're burdened, we can remember Philippians 4:6 and turn our anxieties and requests directly over to You. We affirm that worry is not for us, Your beloved children! We can depend on You to make all things well, deep within our souls. Precious Lord, each time my friend becomes weak and tempted to worry, please help her to remember that Your peace is available in abundance if she will choose to keep her mind on You. Grow the fruit of Your Spirit in her life. In Jesus' name, amen.*

5

My Children Are Rebelling

Thelma, this thing of "train up a child in the way he should go, and when he is old he will not depart from it" is a hoax. I know that sounds sacrilegious, but it sure hasn't worked for me.

I trained up my children in the way of the Lord. I kept them in church from the day they were born. They attended vacation Bible school, Sunday school, the children's and youth ministries, church camp, Bible studies. I taught them the Scriptures in the morning on the way to school. I had them read the Scriptures at night before they said their prayers. Both of them received Christ as their personal Savior before their tenth birthdays. They never acted as if they would do anything but be good children for their entire lives. But something happened when they got into their late teens and early twenties.

They saw me and their dad walk in the faith all the way through their childhood. My goal was to be a Proverbs 31 mother. When my kids were young, they did rise up and call me blessed. They always talked about how my life was a shining light to them. Even when I disciplined them and they got angry with me, they never seemed to resent me. What could have happened to make them go in the directions they are going now? I just don't understand it!

My twenty-one-year-old daughter is living with her boyfriend. My seventeen-year-old son has tattoos all over his body and rings pierced through plenty of places besides his ears. It's a shame to say it, but I look at my children sometimes and wish they were not mine. What are other people thinking when they see them and know how they're living? Sometimes I just want to slap them back into a world I can understand and accept.

Maybe I was too hard on them growing up. Or maybe I wasn't hard enough on them. Who knows? I just don't understand how they could do this to me when I've sacrificed my life for them. My heart is so heavy, Thelma. I am so hurt and disappointed with my children, and I keep wondering where I went wrong.

❧

Girl, you're not alone. How we mothers pine for our children to be perfect! How we want the best for them so much that we grieve when they're not doing what we want, how we want. How we seek for our children to be the epitome of all that stands for good so that people can see they are wonderful and can count us successful as mothers. I understand, Baby, because I'm a mother, too, and a grandmother.

It sounds to me as if you're beating yourself up for somehow failing your children even though you've given mothering your all. You need to stop that right now. Step back for a minute and take a good look at yourself. You are, hear me, *are* a Proverbs 31 woman. Think about who she was. She was industrious, wise, prudent, understanding, focused; she kept her house clean, worked, taught her children, set the example of good, was respected by her husband and children. You are like her.

Are you perfect? I hope not. Because if you are, I'm talking to a dead person. None of us will ever reach perfection until we are released from these earthly bodies of ours. That means that maybe you did make some mistakes while raising your children. I certainly did. I've had to say "I'm sorry" for some of those things. But I guarantee you that none of my mistakes *caused* my children to make some of the decisions they made when they were old enough to decide for themselves.

❧

Remember, we're all in process. Honey, your children are in a process called growing up. As young people mature, they often do things according to the current fads, their curiosity, or their rebellious nature that they know are not right, but they look like fun. Besides that, "everybody else" is doing those things so they must not be that wrong. Don't tell me you never thought like that or stepped off the straight and narrow once in your life!

Your kids, you, and I are all in process. Till the day we die, I hope we will always be learning and growing. Actually, God

38

promises that when He says He will complete the work He began in us (Phil. 1:6). That goes for your children as well because they belong to Him.

Sure, you taught your children about the sanctity of marriage, but your daughter has got to find out for herself with the holy Parent as her teacher. Her current reasoning is probably something like this: "With the divorce rate as it is today, you need to live with somebody before you marry him to see if it's going to work." Girl, we know where that kind of reasoning comes from: Satan himself, the father of lies. What usually happens to Christians who live a lie is that they have no peace of mind. They blame everything and everyone, but the Holy Spirit within them continues to convict them. Eventually, the situation they're in "just doesn't work out" (translation: they can't stand the guilt and consequences anymore). When they find themselves free from that situation, they usually don't get back into the same situation again. They have learned the hard way that God's Word is sure and sin has penalties.

Do you remember the hippie generation? They wore clothes that would shock a harlot. They looked a mess and acted even worse. Many of them who were young rebelled during that time but are productive citizens, business owners, and leaders today. They made it through their innocence and ignorance to maturity. There's hope for your kids!

Not many years ago the spiked, multicolored hair, leather clothes, and army boots were the going things for some of our young people. I will always remember when I was in London waiting for a train, and a young man walked on the platform looking the way I just described. He even had a mean look on his face as if he was saying to everyone present, "Get off my world, I'm coming through." People took one look at him and shrank back.

I was seated on a bench holding the handle of my luggage, so tired I couldn't think. When I saw him coming and people giving him space, I thought, *He's just gonna have to do to me whatever he wants. I'm so tired, I don't even care.*

The young man sat down beside me, still looking as if he could kill somebody. I thought, *I love a challenge. I'll talk to him.* As tired as I was, I said hello and asked him how he was doing. Suddenly, he gave a half smile and answered me, and we began an enlightening conversation that made me think twice about judging someone because he did not look the way I thought he should.

He told me he was a student at one of the universities and explained his studies. I found out how many sisters and brothers he had and what his parents did for a living. We talked about the differences between the accents from the different parts of England and Wales. It was fun!

People stared at us in dismay. I suppose they were thinking, *Look at that old, tired, black, traveling grandma and that weird, no-good, stupid-looking derelict. They make a good match. They deserve each other.* If I had run from him as the others did, I would have missed a marvelous opportunity for cultural enrichment and friendly conversation.

Sweetie, you just cannot judge a book by its cover. Your child whose body is pierced and tattooed is simply following the trends of his generation. I don't like tattoos, but both my son and my grandson have them. Having them has not changed their love for the Lord. Frankly, I think body piercing is ugly. But often surrounding all those holes are people whose growing-up process has not taken away their basic fervor and understanding of who God is. What they look like on the outside does not necessarily reflect who they are on the inside.

Try to keep an open mind and heart where your son is concerned. Don't write him off as a rebel just because of how he looks.

❧

Never stop loving and praying. I believe you should stop thinking about what the Joneses are saying about your children. I mean, check theirs out! Some of them are doing worse than yours. Some of them you haven't even seen lately because they are nowhere to be found.

But none of that is even relevant! The important thing is to show your children you love them by your actions. Don't nag your kids about their choices. If you do, they'll get to the place where they won't want to be around you. They already know how you feel about things. Don't wash their faces with your distaste. Just *love them.*

My friend Barbara Johnson says so well, "When there is no control, there is no responsibility." Baby, you cannot control your grown children. They are no longer babies; at their ages they will continue to make their own decisions, right or wrong. Keep your focus on who your son is becoming inside, not on what he looks like on the outside. Treat your daughter *and* her companion with godly love and respect. Pray for them that God will intervene and change both of their minds. Ask Him to teach them the right way as you have taught your daughter in her youth.

One of the deceased pastors of my church, Dr. Ernest C. Estell Sr., would say, "When your children are little, you talk to them about God. When they are grown, you talk to God about them." I think that's great advice. You can't do much about your children's decisions at this point in their lives, but you can accept them, love them, and pray for them.

❦

Let go. I was feeling like you when one of my children was not acting the way I wanted. I went to God with my churning emotions and asked Him to tell me what to do about it. He spoke to my mind that I was trying to control something I had absolutely no control over. And then He said, "A controlling spirit is a spirit of witchcraft."

I didn't want to hear that! But then He clarified what the scripture "train up a child" really means. It simply means that your children will never forget the training you've given them. Scriptures will pop up in their minds to remind them of their Christian heritage. Because they have given themselves to the Lord, He will never leave them or forsake them. They may attempt to leave Him, but His Word promises that they cannot go anywhere He will not be: "For I am persuaded that neither death nor life, nor angels nor principalities nor powers, nor things present nor things to come, nor height nor depth, nor any other created thing, shall be able to separate us from the love of God which is in Christ Jesus our Lord" (Rom. 8:38–39 NKJV). That doesn't mean that they won't suffer the consequences of their deeds, but praise God, He does not deal with His children according to their sin. Hallelujah!

Mama, you don't have to worry about your children. They are in the best hands ever: God's. I encourage you to remind yourself daily that God Himself is their Parent for eternity, and it is only through His grace and by His power that they can live holy lives. Put your faith in *God*, Sister, not in your children, yourself, or your parenting methods. Park your soul by the refreshing stream of this truth: "God is able to make all grace abound to you, so that in all things at all times, having all that you need, you will abound in every good work" (2 Cor. 9:8 NIV). God is able and eager to give abundant grace to you *and* your babies. Trust Him to do that.

What do you have to do now? Get on with your own life!

Father in heaven, *You are near this mother and her children. You are their Protector, Convictor, Sustainer. Thank You. Sweep over this mama's mind, and free her from the guilt, shame, embarrassment, discouragement, and disgust she feels walking through this period of rebellion with her children. Please give her the strength, patience, tolerance, care, and love she needs to see them safely back to lives of purity and joy in You. Encourage the hearts of all moms and dads in the world today, Father, and help them remember that no matter what is going on in the lives of their kids, You hold every child of Yours in the palm of Your hand. Thank You for being our perfect Parent. Amen.*

6

My Health Is Failing

Thelma, I've been blessed to be healthy all my life. I've never had any sickness more severe than the flu. So when I went to the doctor a few weeks ago for a checkup, I wasn't prepared to hear that I'm not as healthy as an ox like I used to be.

I've been feeling tired and short of breath for the past few months, so the doctor put me through a battery of tests. Turns out my blood pressure and cholesterol are high, my heart didn't fare too well on a stress test, and even my hearing isn't what it used to be.

Thelma, I'm only sixty-one years old. Suddenly, I feel like an old woman. What happened to the healthy body I've always counted on?

That young whippersnapper doctor told me in no uncertain terms that I had to lose weight, rest more, eat right, exercise regularly, and take blood pressure medicine—probably for the rest of my life. I did not want to hear that! She said that if I wanted to live and have a decent quality of life, I had to change my lifestyle. After sixty years, she wants me to change my lifestyle, just like that? Okay, I admit that I've probably taken better care of my car than of my body, but I never used to get sick! I feel as if my body is betraying me.

The worst thing is, I'm starting to feel paranoid. I keep thinking about being sick all the time. Any little pain causes me alarm. I guess I'm willing to eat more fruits and vegetables, take my medicine (much as I hate it), and be more active. But what will I do if none of that works? What if I get worse instead of better?

I'm terrified of losing my health, Thelma. I've witnessed some of the most devout and loyal believers fall to cancer, heart attacks, strokes, back problems, blood disorders, and the like. I love God with all my heart; I am one of His servants. Every day I pray for Him to heal me. But I'm feeling so uncertain about everything these days. The doctor's bad news has really shaken me up.

❧

Honey, I talk to a lot of people with illnesses every week, and I can assure you that everything you're feeling is common and understandable. Sometimes when our health declines and things don't seem to be working out for us, our faith begins to waver. We question God and His promises to us. We think God doesn't care about us and has abandoned us.

That's how Job felt. God's servant was delivered into the hands of Satan and lost everything he had: his children, his possessions, his health. He must have been the worst case of misery and disease I have ever heard of! Thangs didn't look purty from where he sat.

You may think you feel bad, but just listen to this:

> When I lie down I think, "How long before I get up?"
>> The night drags on, and I toss till dawn.
> My body is clothed with worms and scabs,
>> my skin is broken and festering.
> My days are swifter than a weaver's shuttle,
>> and they come to an end without hope.
> Remember, O God, that my life is but a breath;
>> my eyes will never see happiness again.
>
>> (Job 7:1–7 NIV)

Baby, Job was *bummed.*

But in the end, Job decided to trust God, even though it was clear that God was allowing him to suffer. Job was wise enough to accept his plight and wait on the Lord to fulfill his destiny.

God has a plan. I firmly believe that whatever state we're in, God has a plan for us. Even when things appear to be in terrible disarray, "dominion and awe belong to God; he establishes order in the heights of heaven" (Job 25:2 NIV).

Job was a man of God, living for God, loved by God. God could have healed His suffering, baffled servant the first time Job cried out to Him. God could have resurrected Job's children and given his wife a better attitude. But He didn't because He had a plan for Job. God allowed His servant to go through the agony and shame of the most despicable devastation to show Satan and us that even though the body and spirit of a man can be touched by disaster, the man's soul can remain secure in God the Creator. Nothing can separate a godly person from the love of God.

Girl, God has a plan for each of our lives. Maybe this is a part of His master plan for you that you go through this phase of failing health. I know God can heal you, as He eventually healed and restored Job. But is your trust in yourself and your health, or in your Creator?

If God doesn't heal you right now, what will you do? Will you curse God and die, the way Job's wife wanted him to do? Or will you take God at His Word, believing by faith that "the Almighty is beyond our reach and exalted in power; in his justice and great righteousness, he does not oppress" (Job 37:23 NIV)?

❧

Do your part. Even though I believe that God has a plan and is always out for our good, that doesn't mean we should throw caution to the wind and think God is going to protect us from all hurt, harm, danger, and sickness even when we're subjecting ourselves to these things.

For example, people who smoke are putting themselves at risk for all kinds of health problems and diseases. It doesn't matter that they're Christians; people reap what they sow. Often we ask to get sick by the activities we indulge in. Do you think God has anything to do with that? I don't think so! I've learned that I cannot eat certain foods and drink certain drinks because they will upset my stomach. I know what my body patterns are, and I must act prudently to avoid problems.

Besides avoiding exposure to further health risks, you can ask God to help you change your attitude. Girl, at sixty-one, you're simply not going to have the same body you had at thirty-one, no matter what you do! But you can take a positive approach to your health. You can refuse to sit or lie there and let this get the best of you. You can think and talk yourself into being seriously ill or into improving. The choice is yours. Changing your thoughts about your situation will help you adjust to changing your lifestyle. It may not be nearly as hard as you've made it out to be.

❧

Trust in God's healing power. With every generation there are different health problems that take precedence over others. In this new millennium, fighting diseases such as AIDS, influenza, and tuberculosis will be issues. You and I can begin praying now that God will have mercy on us and stop the spread of sickness and disease. Our loving God cares about our well-being. He wants us as healthy as we can be. He heals today, just as He did generations ago. He's the same, yesterday, today, and forever.

Let me tell you what He did for one of my friends. The first time I saw her in the hospital after her automobile accident, she was using a walker and wearing a back brace. Her speech was severely slurred. Every attempt to communicate was a strain. This lady, who had been active as a schoolteacher, minister's wife, community leader, and musician, had become physically and verbally challenged.

For months I watched her struggle with her disabilities and pain. She became depressed by her condition and her inability to get around as she had in the past. But she was a praying woman. She became more determined than ever to walk and talk again.

One day while she was lying in her hospital bed, the Lord spoke to her in her spirit and told her to walk. The doctor came into her room to check on her the morning of her revelation from God. The doctor told her to move slowly and try to sit up in the bed. She told him, "No, sir, I'm going to walk." The surprised physician reminded her that she could not walk. My friend made a bargain with him: "If you get out of my way, I will walk from one end of the hall to the other."

The doctor just watched, stunned, as my friend got up, walked (without help, wheelchair, walker, or cane) up and down the corridor of the hospital. God did it! He healed her! She had the faith. God had the power.

Sister, God has all the power to make you victorious over sickness. The Scriptures say that if there are any sick among us, we should call for the elders of the church and pray in faith for healing. Sometimes God heals instantly. Sometimes He says to wait. Sometimes He says no. Sometimes the ultimate healing is God taking His children home to be with Him. The point is, He's the One in control. I know He always answers prayer. When He doesn't heal as you want Him to, He can give you peace in your mind and heart.

When you pray, my friend, put your faith in God alone. Even if God does not heal you the way you want Him to, will you still trust Him? God's suffering servant, Job, has gone before us to give us an example to follow: "Though he slay me, yet will I hope in him" (Job 13:15 NIV).

Mighty God, *thank You for Your healing power. We realize that You have more healing in the hem of Your garments than all the medicinal care in the universe. You are the ultimate Healer. We thank You for the knowledge You've given to men and women to enable them to diagnose and treat sickness and disease. Please, Lord, empower doctors and scientists to find cures for cancer, AIDS, and all the other diseases that debilitate and kill Your children. And in the meantime, Father, however You choose to heal, help us to accept Your decisions. Encourage my sister, Lord Jesus. Even while her body is suffering, strengthen her mind and spirit. Let her feel You near. Open her eyes to the healthy choices she can make, and help her lay her burdens squarely on Your strong shoulders. Thank You for being the God she can trust. In Your Son's healing name, amen.*

7

I'm in Debt

Money, money, money, money. Thelma, sometimes I think life is all about money. We've got to have it if we're going to eat, dress, communicate, have a roof over our heads, go anywhere, have transportation, furnish our homes, get an education, be safe. Everything requires money, money, and more money.

I used to have a credit card, debit card, charge card, calling card, travel card, traveler's checks, money orders, personal checks, wire transfers, direct deposits, coins, and cash. I thought I was rolling in dough. But the dough I was rolling in was not mine. It belonged to the people who gave me the credit.

When the time came to pay them, my cash was not flowing. When I got the cards, I had a good-paying job, and my husband was gainfully employed. We thought life would be a bowl of cherries for the rest of our lives. Not! We've become intimately acquainted with the terms downsizing, right sizing, outsourcing, *and* termination. *Both of us have experienced all those within the past five years.*

Before we were married, we worked at getting all of our bills paid and being financially stable. So, we entered marriage virtually out of debt. When we built our house, we agreed not to get into debt beyond our mortgage. We were going to purchase furniture as we got the cash to pay for it. Sitting in a house that had only a bedroom suite was fun for a while, but we began to get tired of having no draperies on the windows or pictures on the walls. We were embarrassed to keep asking guests to sit on beanbags. So what did we do? We decided to buy new window coverings and furnish our living/dining area. More furniture called for more accessories. More accessories called for more furniture and fixtures. Before we knew it, we had maxed out two credit cards. But it was okay because we were still working and were able to make the payments.

Then my husband's car broke down. It would cost almost as much to keep patching it up as it would to get another one (we thought). What did we do? We bought another car. It wasn't brand spanking new, but it wasn't a junk heap, either. That meant we had two car notes, maxed-out credit cards, and a mortgage. Add to that electricity, water, gas, telephone, insurance, groceries, gasoline, clothes, personal items, and general upkeep, and we've been living above our means, big time. We've even had to borrow money on another credit card to pay what's due on the others. This is a mess. We have never had major financial problems before. We've never had bill collectors calling or gotten late notices. That's what fills our mailbox now: bills, bills, and more bills.

I'm working for a temporary agency. My husband has two part-time *jobs. We're still not close to what we were making before all these reversals. It's so frustrating and embarrassing to be in this situation. I used to think only deadbeats had creditors looking for them. I have a lot more understanding now. Now I can see why people file bankruptcy. That's not in our plan today, but if this keeps up, it may be tomorrow.*

Thelma, I don't know if we'll ever get out of this mess, but if we do, I never want to be in this situation again. The stress is really getting to me.

❧

Oh, Darlin', do I ever understand where you're coming from! Yes, ma'am. My situation was similar to yours in that I, too, was working and making very good money when I took a terrible financial tumble.

My husband had two successful businesses, and I had been in business for several years making six figures. We had never had a significant financial problem. In the mid-1980s, however, we experienced one *rude* awakening.

The whole economy in Texas went down with the bank failures. All of my business was in the financial services arena because I was a banker in Dallas for twelve years. I was teaching banking students in Texas towns, Chicago, and Minneapolis. The month the banks began to fail started our personal financial avalanche. I lost all my contracts in Texas—85 percent of my gross income—within six weeks.

Like you and your husband, we had never been in debt that we couldn't handle. We didn't know what it was like to have bill collectors breathing down our necks. Things got even more horrible for us after we used up all our savings and still had no income. My husband's small businesses were adversely affected when the local economy failed. With both of us experiencing floundering businesses at the same time, thangs weren't purty!

As I reflect on that uncertain, difficult time, I learned some lessons that might help you too.

❧

Be honest with your creditors. When I found myself facing a critical financial crunch, I wrote to all my creditors and informed them of our circumstances. I wanted to beat them to the draw. When you inform them of your situation, they realize that you are not someone who's trying to rip them off.

Girl, I got on a first-name basis with some of the bill collectors. When they would call me, I would say something like, "Hi there. How's the weather in Delaware? It's pleasant down here. I know you want some money, and I want you to have some money. The problem is, I don't have any. I promise to share with you when I do." If I knew how much I could send them and when, I'd tell them over the phone. If my plans changed, I'd call them and let them know. Nothing beats an understanding!

So, Honey, be nice to the bill collectors, and treat them as your allies rather than your enemies. They have a job to do, but

Girl, Have I Got Good News for You

they're human beings. I was surprised to discover not only that they could be reasonable and long-suffering, but also that some of them seemed to genuinely care about my circumstances. When I treated them with dignity, I usually got the same treatment in return.

❧

Live on a cash-only basis. One thing I am certain of, human nature and opportunity whipped together are not a great combination for staying out of financial trouble. "Easy" credit is very seductive, and too many of us fall into its snare. Having worked in a bank, I know of people who got bill consolidation loans and kept their credit cards to boot. When they paid off their bills with the loan, they'd often stay straight for several months. But almost invariably, they'd go into a store one day, see something they thought they couldn't live without, and purchase it with one of those credit cards that should have been canceled when they got the loan. Girl, it doesn't take but a few times to impulse buy with a credit card before you're right back where you started or worse off because along with the credit card debt you've got the consolidation loan. Yikes!

The fact is, you can't borrow your way out of debt. You've got to pay your way. So cut up all but one of your credit cards (for life-threatening emergencies only). Then follow the advice I once heard: wrap that card in a baggie, and hide it in the back of your freezer under several pounds of ice! From now on, pay cash for anything you buy. It's that simple, Baby: If you don't have the cash, don't get the product.

❧

Ask God to be your CEO. When we found ourselves leaking at the financial seams, my husband and I developed a plan to get our boat afloat again. We agreed to continue to give a tenth to the church, set aside as much as we could afford for ourselves (for saving), and live off the rest. That meant major sacrifices—such as grocery shopping on a full stomach and only with a shopping list! Clothes shopping was completely eliminated until further notice from each other. (Sure glad I bought a nice wardrobe when I had those cards!) Eating out and doing other recreational activities that required money were no-nos. Turning off the lights and stopping the running water became rituals. Everywhere we could tighten the belt, we did.

Girl, it was all worth it. Today, we are financially comfortable again. But much more important, through that dilemma we began to focus even more on the One we belonged to and what we really wanted out of life. We laid all our plans and agendas and dreams at God's feet and asked Him to take over them all. We resigned as the chief executive officers of our own businesses and prayed for God to lead us in the professional and vocational paths He had planned for us. As a result, we found our true calling.

My husband and I now work together in ministry. God almighty is the CEO, and He calls all the shots. My husband is the business manager, which relieves me from dealing with daily fiscal matters. George is good at what he does, and he has time to work on his various automobile and home projects and pass on his expertise to our kids and grandkids. He has an active, full, enjoyable life. As for me, my life is the ministry. When I'm not traveling with Women of Faith conferences or speaking in other places, I'm writing books like this. This is my life's calling.

Baby, your temporary financial troubles can be virtually eliminated if you are serious about making that happen. It will take time, dedication, patience, persistence, tolerance, and determination. We did it. You can too. Just put your mind to it. Develop a plan and stick with it.

Above all else, let this time of financial struggle teach you invaluable lessons you may not learn any other way. Certainly, one of the biggest lessons my husband and I learned is the one stated in Proverbs 19:21 (NIV): "Many are the plans in a man's heart, but it is the LORD's purpose that prevails." God knows I don't ever want to go through financial reversal again (You listening, Lord?), but I'm grateful to have learned what I did. It's such a comfort to George and me to know that God and His purposes are soooo much bigger than all our plans and even our wildest dreams. With Him as our Chief Executive Officer, we are in good hands.

❦

Remember, God is for *you.* Baby, the most important thing for you to remember is that you're not on your own in cleaning up this financial mess. God is on your side! Scripture proclaims this magnificent truth: "'For I know the plans I have for you,' declares the LORD, 'plans to prosper you and not to harm you, plans to give you hope and a future'" (Jer. 29:11 NIV). God doesn't want you in debt, feeling burdened and hopeless! No, He wants to prosper you and give you a bright future.

So confidently ask God to help you be a wise steward over the resources He has given you. Ask Him for favor with your creditors. With you and your husband working together and God on your side, you will have the determination and faith it takes to make your way out of debt and live out His purpose for your lives.

Gracious Lord, *thank You that You have a plan for our lives that includes freedom from financial bondage. Please give us the wisdom and knowledge to cooperate with Your plan for our prosperity. We have not always been prudent in the use of the resources You have entrusted us with, but You are a gracious God who will always make a way where there is no way. You are so good! You have sustained us even after we've messed up and used up money that was not ours. You've given us another chance to make straight what we've done. Please, Lord, help my friend to make the adjustments in her life that will clean up her past and debt-proof her future. Give her all the riches of Your kingdom. In Your name we pray, amen.*

8

My Boss Drives Me Crazy

Thelma, I hate to go to work because my boss is always asking me to do things that are not part of my job description. She hired me for one thing and has me doing ninety-seven more. Whenever I try to say no, she tells me I'm insubordinate and writes me up. I don't think she has one ounce of respect for me.

She drives me crazy with her on-again/off-again communication. Some days I feel that I know what she expects from me, and I try to please her. (Of course, I never hear if she's pleased.) Other days she acts as if I should just be able to read her mind and her moods and practically do her job for her. She is a terrible communicator. I'm not paid enough to put up with this!

My boss avoids doing my annual review until the very last minute. Then on a Friday evening she calls me in and blasts me with negative comments about my performance that should have been called to my attention during the year. Why would she wait a whole year to tell me how she thinks I'm doing? How does she expect me to improve on stuff that I think I'm doing well but she thinks I need to do better?

I've heard from some of my coworkers that my boss talks about me behind my back—how bad my attitude is and how slow I catch on to new things. I think that's very unprofessional. She seems to be the one with the problem. I need to give her an annual review for her personnel file. It won't be nice if I do!

I believe her major objective is to embarrass and belittle me. What's with that? She's got a problem that I really don't know how to deal with. Nothing I do or say seems to get across what I need from her—an understanding. I'd love to just walk in and quit, but I can't, and she knows it.

Thelma, help me deal with this woman, pleeease!

⬤

Baby, I think I understand your situation. My early days of banking bring back similar memories. I had a boss who caused me much agony.

When I interviewed with this woman in the early 1970s, I quickly discovered that she would be trouble. She asked me one of the most stupid questions I've ever heard in my lifetime. "Mrs. Wells," she said, "do you realize that if we hire you, you will have to wait on white people?" My sarcastic response was, "Noooo, you've got to be kidding me." Give me a break! She was still living in the Dark Ages. That was my first clue that she was a dizzy chick.

After I started the job of opening new accounts for customers,

I discovered that one of my supervisor's main goals was to hinder me from learning important information. She apparently wanted to limit my access to what I needed to know so I'd do a poor job and embarrass myself. Girl, that woman did *not* like me! Every chance she'd get, she'd attempt to humiliate me in front of customers by telling me to do something she knew I had not been taught to do. I had not just fallen off the tomato truck. I knew what she was up to.

One day when I was trying to open an account for a sweet older couple, she told me to call a check verification center for information about them. I had never called before and didn't know that the center was automated. I was expecting a live person to answer my call. When the electronic whistles and bells started sounding in my ear, I thought I had called the wrong number. I dialed it again, and once more I did not recognize the tones. I was afraid to ask my boss what to do because I knew that her next move would be to belittle me and make the customers think I was dumb.

When I began dialing the third time, she loudly and rudely commented, "You silly goose! Don't you know what you're doing? Don't you know that every time you connect to that number it costs us money? You are just soooo stupid."

Needless to say, that set me off. Miss Nice Thelma wasn't nice anymore. I went to the department head, who was a great lady, and told her that if she didn't get me away from my obnoxious boss, I was going to drag the miserable woman all over the floor.

Okay, that was not the way to handle it, I admit. I was so angry that I spoke out of turn. However, my reaction got attention.

Now, Baby, *don't do that!* There are more professional and mature ways of handling situations like these. But in my early thirties I was not as anointed as I am now, so controlling my temper in that situation was not one of my virtues. The good that came out of the whole scene was that the great department head lady realized there was a serious problem and she took immediate, legitimate action to straighten it out.

Girl, let me share with you a few things I've learned through the years that might help you in your situation. I hope it comforts you to know that you're not the only employee who has ever felt this frustrated.

Take the initiative. Having to wait on a boss to give an annual review or daily instruction is one of the complaints I hear often from women. Why not try this? It worked for me.

At the beginning of your fiscal year (or anytime you think appropriate), write out a set of goals and objectives for yourself that are in line with your company's objectives. Add to that some of the specific ways you envision meeting those objectives. Then schedule a meeting with your boss to discuss these things, bearing in mind that your boss is mostly concerned about what you can do for the company, not what she or the company can do for you. Remember that in a corporate environment, people are primarily concerned with WIIFM (what's in it for me). You need to take the initiative to show them that you're thinking about this from their perspective and you have a plan.

Throughout the year, make sure you document your performance—the good, the bad, and the ugly. Don't let the boss be the only one who's keeping tabs on what you're doing; *you* keep tabs on *you*. Keep the lines of communication open with your boss and the other powers that be. Instead of waiting passively for your boss to come to you with good or bad feedback, go to your boss. *Ask* her occasionally how you're doing. Ask what you can do to help the department succeed. Find out what you need to do to improve your performance. Even if she will not talk to you right away, write down your questions and ask her for feedback.

Baby, take the initiative to virtually write your own job description and evaluation, and spark conversation about your long-term goals and daily performance. Open and productive dialogue is one of the keys to a successful career.

❧

Create positive visibility. What kind of reputation are you creating for yourself at work? When you draw attention to yourself, is it positive attention? Do your boss and others see you contributing in praiseworthy ways or in problematic ways?

It has been my experience that the squeaky wheel gets the grease. When the squeaky wheel is contributing a good idea or offering to assist others or demonstrating a team spirit, it gets noticed in a positive way. On the other hand, when the squeaky wheel is always complaining, doing a mediocre job, or causing chaos and confusion, it gets noticed in a negative way. Being noticed for what you do wrong instead of what you do right is the surest way to get left behind when it's time for promotions, raises, awards, and so forth.

Creating positive visibility for yourself is every bit as important as doing a skillful job on your daily tasks. So take an honest look at yourself, and see what kind of visibility you're earning. If it's not so appealing to you, you have a choice to let it stay the same (and get the same results you're getting) or change it for the better.

Understand your boss. Some people are motivated by praise and recognition. Some are motivated by straight talk and to-the-point communication. Others are motivated by indulgence of their attention-getting and controlling tendencies. Some are motivated by written proposals; they need time to analyze positions and come to a decision. My point is, all of us are individuals with certain communication styles.

Employees tend to expect their bosses to be concerned with all this and put effort into understanding and motivating their subordinates. And yes, they should do that. But the gate swings both ways. Baby, why not do the same thing for your boss that you'd like and expect her to do for you? You say you want an understanding. Well, let it start with *you* understanding *her*. Study your boss and see what motivates her.

With the supervisor I told you about, after our altercation I decided to look at myself and consider how I could have handled the situation differently. I started studying the boss to see what made her tick. That was a super move for me. Two years later, management made me her supervisor!

Thank God, He had given me wisdom to deal with her gently and compassionately. I had been praying about her and her negative effect on other people. I had asked God to show me how to be a much better supervisor to her than she had been to me. My prayer was that God would give me a pure heart as I related to her.

Shortly after I got that promotion, I moved my former boss into an office that had windows and gave her a more prestigious title. During my "study" of her, I'd discovered that leading subordinates was not her forte. She enjoyed working with people who had a lot of money; she loved rubbing elbows with those folks. So, I gave her a job that allowed her to serve the people she could relate to best.

Girl, that was one of the best decisions I made in my corporate America days. That woman thrived in her new position. Because I had taken the time to understand her, I was able to do what was needed to help her have everything she desired in a job: prestige, power, people she respected. Yes, it would have been really nice if she'd done the same for me, but I didn't have control over that. I decided to put my energy into understanding and supporting her, and that changed everything for me in ways I never could have foreseen.

Baby, if you ask God for help in your situation, He will give you wisdom in dealing with your boss. Take *you* out of the picture, and surrender this whole deal to God!

~

Make God your Boss. Colossians 3:23 (NKJV) tells us, "Whatever you do, do it heartily, as to the Lord and not to men." Girl, that's such good advice! When you remember that the Lord is your ultimate Supervisor and that you're actually working for Him, not people, then you're much more likely to stay motivated no matter what situation you're in. That makes sense to me because He's the One who made it possible for you to work and support yourself with your job in the first place. God's favor! Awesome!

Baby, when God gives us a job, He doesn't do it just because He wants us to work our hind ends off and have material things. Rather, being in the workforce gives us a unique opportunity to shine for Him. Our workplace is a mission field where we get to live our lives before others in a way that pleases and glorifies our Lord.

One way to shine for the Lord at work, especially among nonbelievers, is to remember that everything we do, every assignment we have, is an opportunity to be light in the darkness. People are watching Christians to see how we handle things. Those who don't believe or who are not sure of this Christianity business are always standing on the sidelines watching how we so-called Christians act.

A huge part of being a good employee is being cooperative and willing to go the extra step. Your attitude is 80 percent of your success or failure in life, and perhaps almost 100 percent of your Christian witness at work. When you get angry with your boss for asking you to do things apart from your job description, it would be wiser to graciously accept the task and learn everything you can about it. There might be a written job description for the position you filled, but the fact is, most anything else you're asked to do to benefit the company is a part of your job too. That old adage, "It's not my job," just won't fly in today's corporate environment. It's all your job, Baby. If you were given a year-end bonus, would you say, "Oh, I can't take that; it's not my money"? I don't think so!

Instead of digging in your heels, I encourage you to welcome the opportunity to soak up everything you can. It's to your advantage. I can guarantee you that the knowledge you gain today will help you on your next job tomorrow.

Honey, God already knows exactly what you're going through at work. He sees all and knows all. Going to Him for instructions on how to deal with your work and your boss is your best strategy. While He's working it out for your good, your responsibility is to work happily, heartily, handily, hopefully, and honestly as if you are the one who manages the company and God is the One who owns it. He does, you know. When you trust Him for guidance and wait for Him to show up with it, you will never go wrong. When you take matters into your own hands, you are bound to mess up.

After you've gotten yourself in line with God's plan for your current situation and things still don't work out on this job, trust Him to provide another one. If I were you, however, I wouldn't leave this one without consulting the Chief Executive Officer of your life, the Lord Jesus Christ.

Chief Executive Officer, Sir, *we acknowledge that it is Your will that we work for a living. Thank You for providing jobs for us and giving us the talents, brains, resources, and energy to accomplish them. Lord, You know that the people we work with are not always as sensitive and compassionate, concerned and fair, as they should be. Give us the strength to show them, through our example, how to treat people with respect and kindness. Thank You for knowing every intimate detail of my sister's struggles at work. Please, Sir, give her wisdom and grace in all her dealings. Let the energy she expends be channeled in a positive direction for her benefit and the good of the company where she is employed. Most of all, may this sister and all women around the world embrace their jobs as fertile ground for ministry. Help them to shine the light of Your love into every dark corner. In Jesus' name, amen.*

9

I've Lost a Loved One

Thelma, Thelma, Thelma. Some days I don't think I can make it. Two months ago my son was killed on the night he graduated from high school.

All my children, close family members, and friends were together for the graduation. I'd planned this big get-together afterward to let my boy know how proud I was of him. He had done so well in school and in life in spite of his dad leaving us when my son was young. My boy was president of his class. As a result of his grades, he had been admitted into one of the most prestigious universities in the nation to study premed.

My, was he handsome that day in his cap and gown! There was a twinkle in his eye, and his laughter sounded like music as he leaped and clapped for joy when the principal called out his name. I felt like I would bust with pride as he glided to the stage to receive his diploma.

Everybody came to our house for the big bash. We had such a great time—one of the best times I can remember since my husband left. Along about nine o'clock the crowd started to dwindle, and my son was invited to a party for another graduate. I was fine about his going. His friend had a good family, and I was completely comfortable with his attending the party.

About an hour later, just as my other kids and I were finishing with cleaning up the kitchen, the telephone rang. One of my son's friends was on the line. "Ma'am," he said, "I hate to be the one to have to tell you this, but there's been an accident. Your son is at the hospital, and they need you to come."

My mind started racing. What do you mean, an accident? How is he? What happened? He was just here! Oh, my God!

I could not remember where my shoes were. I told my other children, and they got in a panic, screaming and hollering and asking me questions I couldn't answer. I had to talk to myself and calm down before I could find the car keys. I knew from the sound of my son's friend's voice that something really bad had happened, but I didn't want to think the worst.

When we got to the hospital, we were met by someone I never wanted to see and don't ever want to see again in that context: the chaplain. All I can recall is saying, "No! No! No! No! Let me see my son! This is not happening. Why are you all playing games with me? Don't tell me that my son who I just saw not two hours ago is dead. This can't be. He's just a boy. His life is just beginning. No! I will not accept this. Do something right now! Do you hear me? Do something this very minute! Don't you let him die! Let me see him now. Take me to my boy—right now!"

They tried to calm me down, but it was no use. Finally, I was allowed to see my only son. He was lying there all alone in a cold, isolated little room. He was covered from head to toe with a sheet. I nearly died myself. I thought I was going to die. I wanted to die.

Why him?

Why me?

Why us?

My son was a good son. I'd never had a minute's trouble with him. His future was promising. He was going to be a doctor. He was brilliant, funny, loving, gentle, considerate, handsome. He was a beautiful Christian boy. He hadn't even begun to live.

The doctor came in and told me that when my son was on his way to his friend's house, he was apparently driving very fast up the winding road. There must have been oil or a slick place on the road because his car swerved and plowed into a huge tree. He was killed instantly. It was a one-car accident, a freak accident. Of course, the doctor said he was sorry. Sorry? I didn't want to hear he was sorry. I wanted to hear that my son was going to recover.

The next few weeks were a nightmare. I would wake up every morning thinking that I'd had a bad dream and that my son would knock on my bedroom door, ask to come in, give me a big hug and kiss, and tell me he'd see me later that day. Oh, how I miss that!

Family and friends tried to console me, but some of them just made things worse. People don't know what to say when someone has died. They told me things like, "It's wonderful that he was a Christian because you know where he is." I didn't want him in heaven. I wanted him at home with me! *"All things work together for good."* What was good about my child dying? *"One day you'll be with him forever."* One day was too long to be without him! *"Just think, he didn't have to suffer. God is good."* Why should he have to suffer or die at all? It's not fair. I'm mad at God. *"It's great you have other children. At least they can take his place."* That is so stupid! Nobody can take anybody else's place!

I am so tired of hearing platitudes, I could scream. I don't want to hear another sanctimonious saying or poem about grief. I want everybody to leave me alone. Let me cry. Let me think. Let me try to live through this horror.

❧

Dear, dear sister. I have never lost a child, but I understand that it's the worst experience a person can go through. I am soooo sorry for your losses. My heart aches for you.

I don't want to be like the people who have caused you more pain. I want my words to help you. I certainly won't pretend to know everything you're feeling about losing your precious boy, but I do understand how it feels to lose someone you love.

I lost one of my very best friends when I was in my early twenties. When I heard she had died, I refused to believe it. I got angry and insisted that someone was playing a cruel joke on me. One of my other friends forced me to go to the funeral home to see that she really was dead. I saw her in her casket but could not believe that God would take such a young, vivacious, talented woman. I had just seen and talked with her the night before she died. How could it be?

I had a lot of questions that I didn't ask anyone because I didn't want anyone to think I was questioning God. So, I kept them to myself. It was only after years of maturing and deliberately studying the Scriptures to look for answers to some of my questions that I began to come to grips with what seemed to me a premature and untimely death.

My sainted great-grandmother died more than twenty-two years ago, and I still think of her every day. I still cry sometimes because I miss her so. Granny was sick for weeks before she died. She had always said that she didn't want to continue living when she was not any good to herself or other people. Well, it happened. That final series of strokes took her to that place. My husband, my sister, and a few friends tried to convince me to "let her go" because she had told me how she felt. But every time they would tell me that, I'd get so mad I could spit.

Finally, the Thursday before she died, I sat on my front porch and prayed to God to give me the strength to let Granny go. I even told Him that He could take her. Oh, Baby, that was hard! But I had to release her to the arms of her Father in heaven. Once I released her, I was able to tell her it was all right if she wanted to go home to be with Jesus. The following Sunday at 1:00 A.M., she died.

I didn't cry that night or even at the funeral. But, boy, several weeks after we'd laid Granny to rest I screamed and hollered and bawled and fell on the floor and beat the carpet for what seemed like hours. I knew life would never be the same without Granny, and that hurt soooo much. Today I still talk about her all the time, talk to her in my mind, long for her to be here and to see what a good job she did raising me (ha ha). After more than two decades, her spirit is still strongly with me and will never leave. I tell people she still rules from the grave (and that's a real good thing!).

When my grandfather died, the hardest thing for me to do was to get out of the car and go inside the church to his funeral. The only real father I'd ever had died just minutes after I talked with him on the telephone and begged him to call the doctor. He'd called me and told me he was not feeling well. He had just come inside from mowing his lawn and his arm was hurting. He promised to call me back after he talked to the doctor. When he didn't call back in thirty minutes, I called him back. One of the neighbors answered and told me that the paramedics had just taken Granddaddy to the hospital. I knew he was dead.

As we were approaching the hospital, I told my husband to park in the emergency parking because we would not be there long; my granddaddy was dead. My husband and grandfather were just like son and father. When I said Granddaddy was dead, George got upset with me and told me I didn't know what I was talking about. In silence we entered the emergency area and were met by the chaplain. It all seemed like a very bad dream.

The day of my grandfather's funeral was the hardest day of

my life. I had been to the church a couple of hours before the funeral to take a final look at him before people came to view his body, but when we drove up to the church for the actual service, I refused to get out of the car. I guess it hit me that this would be the last time I would see my grandfather on this earth. It had only been two years since Granny's death. I was losing the people I loved, and it felt like more than I could take. *No! I will not go inside the church! No! This is not happening. All of this will go away, and everything will be back to normal again. If I don't go in, they can't close up his face in that box; they can't have his funeral. I won't have to bury him. No! I will not get out of this car. You can't make me. I'll just sit here forever if that's what it takes.* Those were some of the thoughts I can remember.

Finally, I remember my husband and the funeral director taking me by my arms and literally pulling me out of the car. All the while I was shaking my head, *No, no, I am not going!* I don't remember the funeral service. All I remember is sitting at the grave site, watching them lower that beloved man's body into the ground. I insisted on sitting there until they filled in the dirt.

Baby, it was weeks before I stopped picking up the telephone to call Granddaddy or stopped listening for his call. He died in 1974. I still miss him. I still love him. Even through my tears as I'm talking to you, I recall his wonderful example of fine manhood and thank God for his influence on his little granddaughter's life.

These deaths were in different circumstances at different

times in my life, but all of them were major losses for me. I still feel some of the effects of these losses. You see, Baby, when we are separated by death from the people we love, we never really "get over it." That's a ridiculous expectation. But we can learn to savor the happy times we had with them and benefit from things we learned during the hard times. There was a time when trying to accept the deaths of my loved ones hurt so deeply that I didn't think I would ever recover. But I have. I can laugh and talk about them now without feeling the searing, inconsolable pain of loss. My healing has been a long process, and it started with being honest about all my feelings.

❧

Don't bottle up your grief. The more we can express ourselves, the faster we can heal. Keeping stuff bottled up inside causes other troubles that can push us to the brink of disaster. Sweetheart, I've learned that it's perfectly all right to grieve. Nobody can tell you how long to grieve. Ecclesiastes 3:4 (NIV) says that there is "a time to weep and a time to laugh, a time to mourn and a time to dance." The time is not specified; grieving is an experience unique to every individual.

Some people bounce back from loss relatively quickly, but for others the grief process takes years. The worst thing you can do is to stay strong, pull yourself together, act all right when you're not, and feel guilty when you express your grief. Holding your feelings inside will only make you sick. It's better to cry or rage or beat the carpet or whatever it takes for you to vent your emotions. You will feel anger, frustration, heartbreak, guilt, despair—a multitude of different emotions. These are *normal* feelings, and you need to honor them.

Talk to someone you trust, Baby. If you don't want to vent with your friends or family right now, look into getting involved with a group of people who are experiencing loss. Fortunately, there are grief workshops in many churches and communities designed to help people cope with the grieving process. Few things bring more comfort than sharing with people who *understand*.

And even if you are angry with God, *tell Him*. Guess what? He already knows anyway. I guarantee you that He will not fall off His throne at your announcement. That's the time He can prove Himself faithful to you. So, don't hold anything back, Sweetheart. Express yourself.

❧

Remember, death is not the end. I know this may sound like a platitude right now, but don't throw it out. When I think about my loved ones who have died, I have tremendous comfort in knowing that all of them were Christians. Thinking about that now makes me smile. It lightens my perspective about losing them because I realize that if any of them had a choice to stay with Jesus or come back here, they would all stay where they are.

You've told me that your son was a believer. Believers' approach to death is different from unbelievers'. I have been comforted by knowing that death for the Christian is not the end of life, but a new beginning. Rather than something to be feared, death is a transition to a fuller life. We're relieved from the troubles of this world and clothed with heavenly life and glory. Paul spoke of physical death as sleep where we rest from earthly labor and suffering. It means going to be with our loved ones who've died before us. Just think, your son is in the presence of the living God where there is fullness of peace and joy. Your boy has received a crown of righteousness because he accepted Jesus Christ as his Savior!

None of us wants our loved ones to leave this earth. But when they do, I know without a doubt that their entrance into heaven will be the grandest entrance ever. In all the losses I've told you about and others I haven't, I've known in the back of my mind that my loved ones were with the Lord. With all that was going on in my mind, my heart knew the truth. When I made the funeral arrangements for my relatives, the programs said "In Celebration of Homegoing" because that's exactly where they were going. Through all the tears and pain, the knowledge of their relationship with Jesus Christ was the basis of consolation.

❦

Look forward to the future. Sometimes I try to imagine them up there with Him. I laugh and cry at the same time because, knowing my family, when they're not singing with the angels, they're running around looking for somebody to eat with them at the banquet table. Girl, they did like a dinner party! One day, when I get Home, I'm going to sing with them and have a marvelous meal. I know the day is coming when I will be with them and will *never* be without them again. In eternity, we will all recognize each other, and each of us will be free from pain, heartache, disappointment, tragedy, broken relationships, sickness—nothing will be bad. It'll *all* be glorious. We will be able to shout, "Trouble's over!" when we get Home. Thinking about that gives me joy and hope. My loved ones' spirits are still with me now, but one day they themselves will be with me again. Hallelujah!

> I know that my Redeemer lives,
>> and that in the end he will stand upon the earth.
> And after my skin has been destroyed,
>> yet in my flesh I will see God. (Job 19:25–26 NIV)

In the midst of Job's suffering, he made a poignant statement about death that stands out in my mind. Job's testimony pointed toward Jesus Christ the Redeemer who would come to save the world from sin, condemnation, and final destruction. Because of Christ, we can be free from the dread of death for ourselves and for those we love. When we know that our Redeemer lives in our hearts here on earth and that our relationships will continue and even be greatly enhanced when we get to heaven, we have something to shout praises about!

When you reflect on the past, Sweetheart, savor the good times, cherish the special moments you and your son had together, highlight the things you learned from him, and hold fast to the sweet memories. Remember, after the time for weeping comes a time for laughter. After the time for mourning comes the time to dance for joy.

I declare to you, brothers, that flesh and blood cannot inherit the kingdom of God, nor does the perishable inherit the imperishable. Listen, I tell you a mystery: We will not all sleep, but we will all be changed—in a flash, in the twinkling of an eye, at the last trumpet. For the trumpet will sound, the dead will be raised imperishable, and we will be changed. For the perishable must clothe itself with the imperishable, and the mortal with immortality. When the perishable has been clothed with the imperishable, and the mortal with immortality, then the saying that is written will come true: "Death has been swallowed up in victory."

"Where, O death, is your victory?

Where, O death, is your sting?"

The sting of death is sin, and the power of sin is the law. But thanks be to God! He gives us the victory through our Lord Jesus Christ. Therefore, my dear brothers, stand firm. Let nothing move you. Always give yourselves fully to the work of the

Lord, because you know that your labor in the Lord is not in vain. (1 Cor. 15:50–58 NIV)

———————— ❧ ————————

Dear living God, *thank You for sending Your Son to die so that we may live eternally with You. Thank You that at His death, You conquered death and hell once and for all. Thank You that He has prepared a place for Your children to live eternally with You. We anticipate a day when there is no more sorrow, trouble, or dying. One day we will see You face to face. Hallelujah! But now, dear Lord, comfort my grieving sister. You've promised to fill her broken, empty places with peace, comfort, and joy. I believe You keep all Your promises. Assure her that You are her very present help in trouble. And help her to hold on to the confidence that she will spend eternity with her precious son, just as You spend eternity with Yours. In Jesus' victorious name, amen.*

10

The Hurt Is Too Deep to Forgive

Thelma, how do you forgive someone who has done you great harm? Someone who abused you during what was supposed to be your care-free childhood? Someone else who knew it was going on and never tried to stop it?

How do you forgive your alcoholic father whose behavior was so frightening that it was hard to sleep? You endured all the fussing and disorder in the family, but there was nothing you could do about it because you were too young. You just had to deal with it as best you could, which meant burying it inside you to fester for years. How do you get rid of that kind of burden?

How do you forgive the husband you love when you discover he has been cheating on you for as long as you've been married?

How can you forgive your grown children when they don't call, come to visit, or even remember your birthday?

How do you deal with people who mistreat you on the job by passing you over for promotions when you've been productive and dedicated for years?

How can you forgive the person who is always putting you down and trying to make you feel inferior?

How do you forgive your church members who gossip about you and assassinate your character? Those women are supposed to be Christians.

How do you forgive the people who have spiritually abused you and smothered you with religious legalism that has caused you to wonder if you are even God's child?

How do you put out of your mind the teacher who caused you to lose a coveted award and college scholarship when you graduated from high school just because she didn't like you? You think you've forgiven and forgotten until once in a great while the memory comes back and your heart aches again.

How do you forgive someone who disliked you because of your skin color and went out of his way to make you feel "less than"? How long do you have to grin and bear it?

How do you deal with the disappointment of never hearing the words I love you *from your mother, even from her deathbed?*

How do you forgive a person whom you loved and who promised to live with you until death, but when you got sick and were unable to do for yourself, he told you he didn't marry you to take care of you? How do you deal with living out your life alone?

❧

Oh, Baby, I feel your pain and sorrow, your hurt and anguish. I can identify with you. There have been pains in my soul that hurt so deeply that I never thought I could be healed, let alone forgive the people who harmed me.

For example, there was a time when I hated two people so much that I would get up in the morning thinking about them, go through the day thinking about them, and go to bed at night thinking about them, hating them, wishing they were dead. Those feelings went on for years.

As I look back on those years, I recall being irritable all the time. People would get on my last nerve. I overreacted with my children and other people. I had long periods of low self-esteem. I acted as if everything was fine with me, but I was being eaten up on the inside.

Finally, I got sick and stayed sick for nearly three years. My condition did not improve with medication, bed rest, inpatient care, anything the doctors tried. Every time I thought I was getting better, I'd have a setback.

One day I was confronted by a true friend who told me that she believed I'd get well when I forgave the people I hated. Honey, that didn't sit well with me! I didn't want to forgive. I didn't think it was my job to forgive. I hadn't done anything to those scoundrels. They'd hurt *me*. However, my friend persisted.

After much prayer and Bible study prompted by my friend's insistence, I began to pray that God would help me to *want* to forgive. After a while, I miraculously, found myself wanting to do just that. I was ready to get that load off my chest.

Then I started asking God to give me the opportunity to see the two people I'd hated so I could tell them I forgave them. Girl, watch what you pray for. God hears everything you say! In a matter of days, God brought those people right across my path so I could tell them, sincerely and without strings attached, that I forgave them. A heavy weight was lifted from me the moment I did that. They were shocked and I was relieved. God gets the glory!

❦

Forgiveness is for you. I believe forgiveness is more for you than for the other person. More often than not, the person you are not forgiving is unconcerned about or unaware of your feelings. Who have you hurt by not forgiving? Yourself!

Baby, past hurts cannot be undone. People may still mistreat you. You cannot change a leopard's spots, but you can change *your* design. I remember what an older preacher once said to me: "You are not responsible for how people treat you. You are only responsible for your response to them." Now, that'll preach!

Patsy Clairmont says eloquently, "We cannot allow the conduct of someone else to dictate our future." So true! When you fail to forgive anybody of anything, you allow him to determine the quality of your life. He controls you whether you want to admit it or not. The only sensible, Christian thing to do is to put the situation into the hands of the Lord and let Him wash you with the water of forgiveness. Forgiveness is work. But it's worth the doing. When you really forgive, the snake still bites, but the poison doesn't penetrate.

❧

You can't forgive in your own power. When you've been wounded, it's hard to welcome the antiseptic of forgiveness so you can heal. You may not want it. You want to hurt the people who've harmed you. You want to see them hurt as badly as you are hurting. In fact, they ought to hurt worse than you do. So you hold on to the hurt, rehearsing it day after day, month after month, year after year. Every time you play it back on the video of your mind, it intensifies. It becomes more and more ingrained in your spirit until it makes you sick.

Baby, forgiving is too hard for us to do by ourselves. We'll never make it if we do. Only the Spirit within us is holy enough to replace the poison of bitterness with the balm of forgiveness. Only when you give the situation to God and let Him heal you can you hope to find relief.

I suggest that you start moving toward healing by praying, as I did, for the willingness to be willing. It doesn't matter how far you are from that willing place right now; it's God's business to sanctify you in His perfect time. Just tell Him that you are tired of feeling so burdened and that you want to be released. Let me pray this prayer of Paul over you right now:

Now may the God of peace who brought up our Lord Jesus from the dead, that great Shepherd of the sheep, through the blood of the everlasting covenant, make you complete in every good work to do His will, working in you what is well pleasing in His sight, through Jesus Christ, to whom be glory forever and ever. Amen. (Heb. 13:20–21 NKJV)

If you really want God to work in you like this, Baby, I encourage you to ask a couple of your believing friends to pray this prayer over you as well. Tell your friends that you want to heal from your pain and have the peace of God through Jesus Christ. Scripture tells us that where two or three believers are gathered together in His name, He's right there in their midst (Matt. 18:20). Let Him come to you and dwell richly with you until He fills you so full of Himself that there's no more room for your bitterness.

❧

Let God judge. One of the reasons we hold on so tightly to anger and bitterness is that we're afraid those who've hurt us will "get away with it" if we let go. I know that was true for me. If I didn't keep replaying in my mind all the things the people I hated had done to deserve my wrath, then I might forget, they might forget, and their dastardly deeds would go unpunished.

Well, guess what? Those two sure weren't sittin' around thinkin' about what they'd done or feelin' bad about it—and they weren't gettin' "paid back" from the misery I was creating for myself. I was the only one suffering!

I think one of the most humbling and comforting passages in Scripture is 1 Corinthians 4:4–5 (NIV). Paul said, "My conscience is clear, but that does not make me innocent. It is the Lord who judges me. Therefore judge nothing before the appointed time; wait till the Lord comes. He will bring to light what is hidden in darkness and will expose the motives of men's hearts. At that time each will receive his praise from God."

Oh, Baby, that gives me such relief and hope! It's not up to me to judge anything or anyone, not even myself. I'll always get it wrong. God guarantees that He'll sort out everything according to His perfect insight and justice. I don't have to burn up any more energy seeking revenge or trying to expose people's wickedness. That's God's job! He'll do it all in His own good time. Meanwhile, I just need to get on with my life.

I hope you can let God decide how the people who've hurt you should be judged and dealt with so you can heal and change your focus. Life is short, Sweetie. I know it has caused you great pain, and my heart goes out to you. But don't keep hurting *yourself*. Open your heart to the One who can fill it with the balm of forgiveness. No wound is too grave for Him to heal.

O Divine Master, *grant that we may love others as You love us; that we may forgive trespassers as You forgive us. It is a part of Your perfect plan that we have forgiving hearts that are holy and acceptable to You. Give my sister a forgiving heart, Lord. Free her from the chains that link her to the horrors of the past. Lead her forth in victory, relieved of the burdens of bitterness and haunting pain. Thank You, Sir, for hearing and answering our prayer in perfect faithfulness. In the name of Your Son, Your ultimate sacrifice, amen.*

11

I'm Struggling with an Addiction

Thelma, I've got this monkey on my back that won't let go. I have been a drug addict for more than ten years. I started using marijuana when I was in elementary school. I've done everything from smoking pot to popping pills, to shooting up and snorting coke and smoking crack. I've been in and out of drug rehabs, hospitals, even mental institutions, and nothing works.

I feel so bad because I've taken everything my parents had of value and sold it for stuff. I've taken parts off cars and pulled plumbing out of houses to support my habit. I've even gone so far as to prostitute myself for a fix. My children have been taken from me because I left them by themselves so much that the neighbors called Children's Services. I'm on probation now for possession of a controlled substance. I hate this! I'm sick of this! I want out of this!

My parents have exhausted all their resources trying to get help for me, but within a few weeks or months, I'm always right back where I started. Drugs are so easy to get. I can't resist. It's like a powerful

*magnet pulling me to it all the time. In the middle of the night I've
got to go out and find it so I can sleep. That's all I think about. That's
all that matters to me anymore.*

*I don't know what to do. Sometimes I feel like killing myself.
Then it would be over, and I wouldn't have to worry about any of
this anymore. You may not believe me, but I love my parents. I love
my children. I hate myself for what I'm doing to them.*

❧

Well, Honey, you *are* in a mess. I've never been in the fix you're
in, but I've had enough exposure to the issues surrounding substance abuse that I believe I can steer you in the right direction
if you really want help. I've been a board member of one of the
most successful drug centers in Dallas, and I've attended drug
counseling sessions for my own benefit. Most of all, I've dealt
with drug abuse in my own family.

Let me be frank with you, if you are not ready to accept what
I'm going to say, then don't waste my time. I *want* to help you,
but my wanting to help you isn't the point, is it? The question is,
Do you really and truly want help? I have learned that an addict
has to "hit bottom" before she gets serious about recovery. Every
recovering substance abuser, alcoholic, or food addict has a story
to tell about bottoming out over the addiction and its consequences. If you've reached that point, then we can talk.

❧

Admit that you're whipped. It sounds to me that you've already taken the first step toward being helped: you are no longer in denial about your problem. You have called it what it is—addiction. Because you've been in rehabs, you know the physical ramifications of crack and other drugs. They attack your central nervous system the very first time you use them, causing you to want more and more. That first high is the best high you will ever get, but you are constantly trying to recapture that initial rush. These drugs have gotten into your bloodstream, and just as the potato chip commercial says, "You can't eat just one."

Besides the very real physical dependency you're experiencing, you've developed a powerful emotional affair with the drugs. You're hooked. You feel that you can't live or be at peace without your supply. You can't imagine daily life without your reliable, predictable "best friend." Am I right?

Honey, this kind of physical and emotional dependency is a lot bigger than you are, stronger than your parents' love for you or your love for your own children, more tenacious than your own puny will. And don't fool yourself into believing that you can just "think" yourself out of addiction, either. Positive thinking without the Spirit of God controlling your thoughts is like a beautiful song played on a tape recorder that is badly in need of cleaning.

Baby, if you are holding on to even a molecule of the delusion that you can get better through any self-determination, loving relationship, or human method or program, it's time to let go once and for all. Only God can deliver you from self-destruction.

Place your trust in Christ alone. Some of the most successful reha-bilitation facilities take you through a twelve-step program, which emphasizes that you are not in control of you; there is Someone bigger than you working in you to control you, to help you, to heal you. No people I've known who have been set free from addiction have been delivered by a drug rehab, even though the programs in rehab were the instruments God used to facili-tate their healing. Their liberation was a result of becoming aware of what was happening inside them, studying and believ-ing God's Word, praying for deliverance, and believing that God would rescue them from themselves.

God's Word promises that He is "able to do immeasurably more than all we ask or imagine, according to his power that is at work within us" (Eph. 3:20 NIV). That promise can give you great hope and anticipation on your own journey. You have said that the drugs you take are powerful and draw you to them like a magnet. But, Baby, there is a Greater Power who wants to knock out the villain of drugs in your life. The Holy Spirit of God is at work within you right now—ready, willing, and able to take away your need and urge for drugs and to set you free from the thought of drugs once and for all.

First John 4:4 (NKJV) proclaims that "He who is in you is greater than he who is in the world." That Greater Power sent you to me today. That Power has been protecting you from harm and death. That Power enfolds you, consoles you, and wants to heal you right now. Sometimes that Power delivers instantly. Sometimes He takes you through a process of healing and deliverance. The fact is, Jesus Christ through the power of the Holy Spirit wants you clean and sober forever. Trust Him to deliver you now.

❦

Believe that God loves you unconditionally. Baby, the most important thing for you to know as you trust God for healing is that He loves you, *no matter what.* You are a wonderful person planned by God, loved by God, and wanted by God. Your addiction does not negate how God feels about you. First John 4:9–10 (NIV) assures you: "This is how God showed his love among us: He sent his one and only Son into the world that we might live through him. This is love: not that we loved God, but that he loved us and sent his Son as an atoning sacrifice for our sins."

Just as God loves you, you must begin to love yourself enough that you will do whatever it takes to get clean and stay clean. Baby, let's recognize what's really happening. The drugs are not necessarily the problem; your feeling about you is really the problem. Sometimes the biggest obstacles standing in the way of a person's recovery are her self-hatred and her unwillingness to recognize her value to the Creator. When we believe we're worthless, we act accordingly. Satan's favorite tool of our self-destruction is convincing us that we are unlovable and that God has given up on us. Girl, if the enemy has you convinced of that diabolical lie,

I urge you to bathe your mind in the truths of Scripture. Read every verse about God's love you can find, and commit your favorites to memory. Resist the devil and he will flee from you (James 4:7)!

If you're ready to take the next step, I encourage you to sign *yourself* into another drug rehabilitation center and make up your mind that you are serious about recovery. Don't do it for your parents, your children, or anybody else. Do it for you. Because, Girl, you're priceless to God.

———————————— ❧ ————————————

Father in heaven, *the One who knows all about us, thank You for knowing the thoughts and desires of this precious daughter of Yours. Lord, I have seen You deliver people from addiction. I have watched You forgive them of their sins and wash them as white as snow. Lord, I have witnessed their continual deliverance as they lead productive lives after years and years of bondage. Lord, You don't love them any more than You love this precious woman! Father, please release her from the clutches of addiction. I trust You right now to do that. Together we speak to the strongman of addiction and call it out by the power of the Holy Spirit. We proclaim that it will never torment her again! The strongman of addiction must fall under subjection to Jesus Christ and the blood He shed on the cross. Father, please cover Your daughter with the matchless blood of Jesus. Break her bonds and set her free. In the power of Jesus' name, amen.*

12

I Married an Alcoholic

Thelma, I need to talk with you about my husband. I knew before we married that he drank a lot with his buddies, but I thought he was just a social drinker. I was floored when he came to our wedding drunk! Our wedding night was a disaster. I thought it was because he was nervous, and everything would soon be all right. Little did I know that my husband is an alcoholic.

During the first few years of our marriage, he was just drinking on the weekends with his friends. Then it got to be every evening when he came home from work. Soon he began stopping at the club or playing dominoes every night after work. How he still functioned on his job, I don't know.

When my husband is drunk, he often accuses me of cheating on him. Our sex life has become very strained because I don't want to be intimate with someone who smells like a brewery all the time. The more distant I've become, the more hostile his accusations have become. If I'm not home when he thinks I should be, he calls around asking my friends and family members whether they've seen me. I can't even go to the grocery store without him paging me.

Now he's started calling me names and verbally abusing me. Recently, he even had the gall to try to fight me physically. My daddy didn't hit me, and I'm sure not going to let a drunk man beat on me! When he came after me, I managed to hit him a good one and get out of the house.

I believe our children are getting scared of their dad. They often ask me if we have to live with Daddy. It breaks my heart that our children would rather live without their father. When I try to talk to my husband about what's happening, he gets defensive and belligerent and says I just want to get rid of him so I can have someone else.

I've talked to some of my girlfriends about my situation, and their advice is all over the map. Some say I need to just accept my husband, for better or for worse. Others tell me to leave and never look back. Take my children and start a new life. That may be easy for some people, but I've always believed that children need both parents.

Another friend told me that maybe I was being punished for something I'd done in the past. I'm glad I was at a point where I could tell her, "Don't even go there. Everything I've done wrong in the past, I prayed to God to forgive me, and He did. God has already forgiven me, and He doesn't wash my face with it!"

But, Thelma, I don't want to live like this. I love my husband, but I don't like him anymore. He's really a good person when he's not drinking. He never treated me like this when he was sober. I want my marriage to work, but it's dying more and more every day.

I don't know what to do. My mother suggested that I go to an Al-Anon meeting or some other program and see what they have to offer. What do you think?

❦

Sweetheart, I agree with your mother. Alcoholism is a complex physical and spiritual disease, and I believe it is necessary to get outside help in dealing with an alcoholic and the confusing family dynamics created by living with one. Practicing alcoholics typically deny that they have a problem. They are prone to mood swings. They accuse other people of doing wrong to cover up their own wrong. Over time, they tend to get violent. They lie. They try to hide their liquor. Sometimes they become paranoid. A nonalcoholic can't begin to deal with all that without getting pretty nuts herself. That's why alcoholism is considered a family disease: it involves and affects everyone, not just the drinker. You know I'm right from your own experience.

❦

Change what you can. In twelve-step programs such as Alcoholics Anonymous and Al-Anon, one of the first things members are taught is a prayer that works wonders in restoring mental and spiritual balance:

> *God, grant me the serenity to*
> *accept the things I cannot change,*

> *the courage to change the things I can,*
> *and the wisdom to know the difference.*

Although you can't control your husband's drinking no matter what you do, you can change some things about your situation. One of my best friends has been in your shoes. All the things your husband is doing, my friend experienced. For a long time she just existed from one day to the next. She took care of the house and centered her life on her children. She was a classic enabler because wherever her husband fell short, be it in parenting, dealing with finances, or showing up for life, she picked up the slack. She would call in sick for him on his job, make excuses for him when he was absent from family gatherings. She had to hide her purse from her husband because he would steal money. Along with the drinking, he started gambling.

After seven years of existing and enabling, my friend became angry with her husband and stopped putting on a facade for the family. She got more involved in church, her children's school activities, and community affairs. Within a few months, her husband followed his family to church and "rededicated" himself to the Lord. That lasted about a month. The only reason he went to church was to keep an eye on his wife.

❧

Change your focus. My friend refused to blame herself for her husband's behavior. One thing is sure: *you are not responsible for grown folks.* Instead, my friend prayed for God to give her wisdom in dealing with her husband.

One day, quite unexpectedly, the Lord spoke to her spirit and told her to change her focus. God urged her to focus on *Him* instead of on her alcoholic spouse. As she obeyed and put her energy into growing closer to Jesus, God graciously opened her eyes to how critical it was for her to stop being part of the problem of alcoholism in her home and instead become part of the solution. She had to realize that her husband needed help she couldn't give, and rather than focusing on him and trying to get him straight, she needed to take care of herself and her children.

Changing her focus took my friend out of her comfort zone. Denial swooped in, and she wanted to believe that her husband was not as bad off as he really was. When he went on a drinking binge, she'd get upset; he'd bring her something nice; she'd accept it and keep hoping against hope that this would be the last time he would get drunk. Not! She stayed in that crazy-making situation for a long time, waiting on God to reveal to her what to do next.

My friend and I prayed regularly about her family's situation. One day when we were traveling together, she stopped in her tracks and told me, "I'm moving out when we get back. I must face the facts about him and get out of a losing situation. He won't get a decent place for us to live. He never has any money to pay for anything. We have children in college, and he's given them a whopping two hundred dollars since they've been there.

I know what the Bible says about divorce. I don't have any intention of divorcing him, but I am moving away from him. I just don't believe God intended for any of us to take the verbal and physical abuse, the neglect, and the disrespect that I'm getting from him. I love him and would do anything to help him. Maybe this is the first step."

Sweetheart, I really can't tell you what to do. I can tell you that my friend is looking better, smiling more, enjoying peace and quiet in her own place, building a bank account. Her children have finished college, and she's enjoying work and stopping to smell the roses along the way.

❧

Trust God for the results. As a Christian, you have all the wisdom of the universe available to you. James 1:5 (NIV) instructs us, "If any of you lacks wisdom, he should ask God, who gives generously to all without finding fault, and it will be given to him." So, Baby, ask God what to do. He will speak to you as He did to my friend. Every situation may have a different result. God knows best. The safest place in the whole wide world is in the perfect will of God.

Psalm 120:1 (NIV) has been a refuge scripture for me and many others. I believe it will help you too. It says, "I call on the LORD in my distress, and he answers me." We can always rest assured that God hears our prayers and comes to our rescue. He chooses the way He will rescue us. Our responsibility is to have faith in Him and do what He says. God understands everything about you, your husband, your family, and your circumstances. God knows exactly how to speak to you so you will have no doubt that it's Him. Trust Him and never doubt. He will surely bring you out.

Ever-present God, it blows my mind that You know all about us. You know where we are, what we need, and how to deal with every situation. Thank You, Father, that You have a plan for my sister in Christ. Thank You that when she asks, You will reveal to her exactly what to do in Your perfect timing. Lord, You are able to release her husband from the bonds of alcoholism. Please work in his life right now! Father, I also pray for a hedge of protection around my friend and her children. Please keep them safe. Enable them to be part of the solution to this disease rather than part of the problem. We plead the blood of Jesus on their circumstances and know in our hearts that You are the mighty Rescuer. In Jesus' name, amen.

13

My Husband Left Me

Thelma, for thirty-seven years I was married to the same man. The first man I had ever been intimate with. My first love. My high school sweetheart. The man of my dreams. The father of my children. The man I bought two houses with and shared a bank account with. The man I supported through school and pushed to succeed in his career. A man I thought loved the Lord because he taught Sunday school and participated in church activities. A man who loved life and loved to laugh. A man who knew how to be serious and how to play. My husband. My life.

I never dreamed that one day he would look me straight in the eye and tell me he didn't love me anymore. He was getting out. He was tired of pretending because he hadn't loved me for a very long time. There was nothing left, he said. I was a good woman but not one he wanted to spend the rest of his life with.

Thelma, I simply could not believe my ears. It had to be a bad joke. Surely, he was going to tell me he was teasing, and we could get back to normal. This just couldn't be! What happened? What did I say? What did I do? What was I going to do?

My husband went to our room, packed his bags, left me some money on the dresser, loaded up his car, and drove into the sunset. I was in shock! I simply could not comprehend it! I stood in the kitchen in a daze. What in the world just went on here? *I didn't know what to do. All I remember was that I sobbed and sobbed until I fell to the floor with a throbbing headache, and all I could do was beat the floor. It must have been hours before I got up.*

I didn't feel that I could call anybody. The only thing I could tell anyone was that my husband left me. There was no explanation. What was I going to tell our children? How was the church going to deal with me? Who knew about this besides me? There must be some other woman. Who is she? Do I know her? He never acted as if there was anybody else. He never acted as if anything was wrong.

How could he do a thing like this when I've devoted my life to him? *I thought.* Who does he think he is anyway? He's no spring chicken. He'll be back. When he finds out that nobody wants an old dog, he'll be barking back to me.

That's what I thought. It has been two years now. He's not back. We have not gotten a divorce because I refuse to give him one. I will not free him to go on with his life after he has ruined mine. No way! I'm suffering, and he has to suffer too. I'll show him. By the time I get through harassing him, he'll wish he'd stayed. Fool! I like seeing him squirm. He was nuts to leave me 'cause I'm not ever going to let him forget it. I'll get my revenge if it's the last thing I do on this earth.

❦

Sister Girl, either you're still in love with that scoundrel or you've allowed hatred to taint your whole approach to this situation. Just listening to you talk about your husband makes me think that you're holding on to hope against hope. You still want him back and think that focusing on him will keep him in your sight and you on his mind. Or you hate him so much for hurting you that you want him to suffer for the rest of your life and his. You call him names, wish him misery, harass him, and refuse to give him a divorce.

Which is it, Baby, love or hate? More important, who is this all about? The question is not, What's happening to him? The real question is, What's happening to you?

The only thing I know to do is to tell you what I believe is right. Will you hear me out?

❦

Pour out your heart to God. As I listen to you, I can hear your stress and tension. I can imagine the sadness and bitterness in your eyes. I see a hurting woman who has allowed someone else's decisions to kill her joy. I see someone taking responsibility for someone else's choice. I see someone determined to make life torture for the person who hurt her. I see a dying soul!

Honey, God's Word is full of the laments of God's people.

You are not the first to feel this anguish. Can you relate to the words of the psalmist who was betrayed?

> If an enemy were insulting me,
>   I could endure it;
> if a foe were raising himself against me,
>   I could hide from him.
> But it is you, a man like myself,
>   my companion, my close friend,
> with whom I once enjoyed sweet fellowship
>   as we walked with the throng at the house of God.
>
> (Ps. 55:12–14 NIV)

I encourage you to spend some time in the Psalms, letting the laments of God's servants speak to the pain and bitterness in your heart. When I'm in the dumps, it always comforts me to know that I'm not the first or the only one to feel just this way—and worse. God can handle every ounce of the anguish in our souls. Jesus is the Man of Sorrows; He's acquainted with grief. He has carried all our heartaches and borne all our pain (Isa. 53:3–4). He's there for you, Baby. Pour out your heart to Him.

❧

Focus on your life. Next, let's stop talking about your husband and what you once had with him. Right now it ain't about yo' husband; it's all about you. That joker is gone. He may never come back. Face reality. The day he walked out is the day he died from your relationship. It has been two years now. If it's dead, bury it.

During the past two years, did you ask God to restore your marriage? Did you study your Bible about marriage and how God can restore and reconcile people to each other? Or did you turn your back on God and pretend He doesn't exist? We know that God wants to and can restore broken relationships, but it has to be the desire of both parties to make this happen. Even if your husband has second thoughts about leaving, will treating him badly help him decide to return to you? Actually, what have you gained by mistreating him? Girl, two wrongs never make a right!

Honey, it's time to stop focusing on your husband and start focusing on yourself. You can't control him. No, none of this is fair, and you don't have to like it. But God has given you your own life to live.

❧

Recognize your opportunities. Start by taking a good look at where you are right now. You are virtually single. You have an opportunity to free yourself from your marriage vows because your husband abandoned you. You have a chance to go on with your life and make it whatever you want it to be. You are in the prime of your life with many years to enjoy. You have health and strength and are independent. You know the Lord. Girl, you have everything going for you to help you get up, get out, and get on with your life.

You're in a position to make choices—choices that can determine the quality of your life from this day forward. Choosing to berate, belittle, and beguile your husband will only steal your life. Choosing to forgive him, pray for him, and let him go will not only release him, but will release you as well. You are bound by your own actions. *You* are holding you back. You are creating your own pain.

What can you change? Not him. Not what other people think. But you can change your whole approach to this agonizing turn of events. You can start paying attention to your life and living it to the very best of your ability. You can let go of your husband and let God deal with him. What a relief!

❧

Let God take care of His own business. You need to understand that you are too important and valuable to yourself, your family, and God to waste your life in pursuit of revenge. Pay attention to Romans 12:19 (NIV): "Do not take revenge, my friends, but leave room for God's wrath, for it is written: 'It is mine to avenge; I will repay,' says the Lord."

Friend, you don't have to worry about your husband being paid back for hurting you. That's God's business. You are not responsible for how people treat you; you are responsible only for how you respond to them. Your only job now is to love and obey God. His Word instructs you to love those who do harm to you and spitefully use you. Did you know that when you do that, you make them feel worse than when you try to get them back? Paul taught us in Romans 12:20 (NIV):

> If your enemy is hungry, feed him;
> if he is thirsty, give him something to drink.
> In doing this, you will heap burning coals on his head.

The choice is yours, Sweetheart. If you want your spirit to remain sick, keep on trying to get revenge. If you want the joy of the Lord restored to you and your spirit released to find happiness again, give it up. Go on with your life.

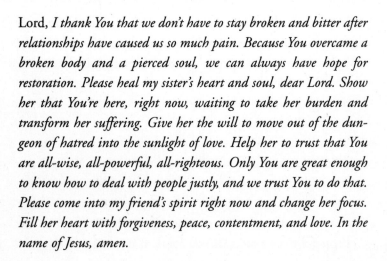

Lord, *I thank You that we don't have to stay broken and bitter after relationships have caused us so much pain. Because You overcame a broken body and a pierced soul, we can always have hope for restoration. Please heal my sister's heart and soul, dear Lord. Show her that You're here, right now, waiting to take her burden and transform her suffering. Give her the will to move out of the dungeon of hatred into the sunlight of love. Help her to trust that You are all-wise, all-powerful, all-righteous. Only You are great enough to know how to deal with people justly, and we trust You to do that. Please come into my friend's spirit right now and change her focus. Fill her heart with forgiveness, peace, contentment, and love. In the name of Jesus, amen.*

14

I Can't Believe I'm Divorced

When I said, "I do" I meant, "till death do us part"! I thought my husband felt the same way. But I question that now, Thelma. I question everything.

When we were dating, I often wondered whether marrying him was the right thing to do. Those doubts lingered even on our wedding day. Although he was articulate, artistic, brilliant, nice looking, flamboyant, and popular, I always had a niggling feeling that something wasn't right. I knew there were some flaws in his behavior. Sometimes he didn't keep his word. He was slightly undependable. Occasionally, he became defensive when I asked him certain questions about his whereabouts or activities. His credit was bad when we got married. I tried to help him straighten it out and almost got mine tangled up with his.

Much of our married life was spent with him telling lies and covering up for his activities. He would stay away from home for several days at a time without any explanation. When he'd come home, he had the nerve to walk back into the house as if nothing had happened. This went on for months. Finally, I issued him an ultimatum: "Either get your life straight and be a full-time husband, or the next time you're gone, you're out of here on your ear with just your clothes, the few things you brought into this marriage, and the wedding gifts your family gave you!"

He promised that it was the last time he would ever deceive me. He said he would never stay away from home again. Oh, yes, he promised the moon, sun, and stars. You know what? He kept that promise for several months. Then the moon got dark, the sun faded, and the stars fell out of the sky. He didn't come home for a week.

I decided it had happened for the last time. I had to make a point! I had to keep my promise!

After this last disappearing act, he came home to find the locks and the security code changed. I announced to him through the closed door that I was going to file for divorce that very day. He did not argue or try to stop me. So I filed for divorce on the grounds of abandonment.

In a little over sixty days, with no contest from him, we were divorced. It was too easy, Thelma. Nobody tried to stop me. He didn't put up a fight. He agreed to everything. Am I supposed to feel rejected? Frankly, I don't. I just can't believe I'm divorced.

Thelma, how can people be so in love when they get married and so out of love before they finish paying for the wedding? When I got married, getting a divorce was as far from my mind as jumping out of an airplane and expecting to fly. But here I am now, a divorce statistic. We were married only twenty-eight months. It's hard not to feel disillusioned.

❧

Honey, marriage ain't all it's cracked up to be. We have all been sold the storybook edition of marriage that says, "And they lived happily ever after." We take it literally to mean there will never be a problem. We fail to realize that whenever there are two people in any kind of relationship, things are not going to be a bowl of cherries all the time.

When my three children were talking about getting married, one thing I told each of them to remember was, "If there's something about your prospective spouse that you can't stand now, multiply that one thousand times, and that's how bad it's going to feel after you are married. Don't get married thinking you will mold your spouse into your image. It won't work! You can't change anybody. I don't care how good he looks to you now, you'll wake up one morning, look at him, and think, *What in the world have I done? I can't stand him today!* That doesn't mean you don't love him. It means that the things you don't like about him are really getting on your nerves and you can't do a thing about it. So be careful about choosing a spouse. If God didn't put you together, don't you get together."

As you've discovered, the qualities in your husband that concerned you all along only got worse after you were married. You chose to close your eyes to the truth before you said your vows, and you both paid a high price.

Fortunately, that's not the end of the story. It never is for a child of God!

❧

Let go of guilt. God has said He hates divorce (Mal. 2:16). He also hates lying, stealing, cheating, backbiting, abuse, bitterness; I could go on and on. But for everything He hates, He offers forgiveness when we ask for it. God's grace is sufficient for *all* the mistakes we make. Girl, is that good news or what?

Jesus said, "Come to Me, all you who labor and are heavy laden, and I will give you rest. Take My yoke upon you and learn from Me . . . For My yoke is easy and My burden is light" (Matt. 11:28–30 NKJV). Beating yourself up because of your choice to get a divorce is like crying over spilled milk. When it's spilled, it needs to be wiped up. You made a choice, good or bad; now you need to wipe up the mess and move on with your life.

The heavy burden you're imposing on yourself can be removed by the power of almighty God when you submit it to Him. Give it to Jesus! Ask the Lord to take away all your hurt, pain, guilt, embarrassment, and despair. Tell the Lord that you don't want those burdens anymore. Ask Him to forgive you of any and all mistakes you've made. Then *believe* He will forgive you and not bring it up to you anymore. No mess is so big that God cannot clean it up!

Stay open. I know you never want to go through this kind of hurt and disappointment again. I'm sure it would be tempting for you to shut down all your emotions and isolate yourself from relationships. But, Honey, God created you with an innate longing for intimacy, and trying to kill that off is not the answer to your fear and disillusionment.

As a woman of God, you can always claim grace for today and hope for tomorrow. You know why? Because God is absolutely faithful, even when we are not. When we are ready to move on from a place of discouragement and defeat, God is right there to shower His love on us and make all things new. No, it doesn't always happen overnight. But I guarantee you, Baby, if you wait on the Lord and place your trust in Him, He will restore your joy and give you fresh vision for the future.

I urge you to keep your heart open, rebuke negative thoughts in the name of Jesus, and meditate on God's Word. Start with these wonderful verses from Lamentations:

> I remember my affliction and my wandering,
>> the bitterness and the gall.
> I well remember them,
>> and my soul is downcast within me.
> Yet this I call to mind
>> and therefore I have hope:

Because of the LORD's great love we are not consumed,
> for his compassions never fail.
They are new every morning;
> great is your faithfulness.
I say to myself, "The LORD is my portion;
> therefore I will wait for him."
The LORD is good to those whose hope is in him,
> to the one who seeks him;
it is good to wait quietly
> for the salvation of the LORD. (Lam. 3:19–26 NIV)

Then, find some single Christian friends who are striving for the same relationship with the Lord that you are. Bond with them so you can talk to and socialize with people who understand your situation. Encourage one another to stay openhearted and emotionally alive because, Girl, that's what life is all about.

Most of all, open yourself wide to the presence of the Holy Spirit in your life. Ask God to make you a wise, discerning woman. Ask the Spirit to guide you into all truth, and then follow His guidance wholeheartedly. He will never lead you wrong.

Fall in love with Jesus. Before you begin any other relationship, please, Honey, fall madly in love with Jesus! Memorize verses that inspire you and hide His Word in your heart that you may not sin against Him (Ps. 119:11). Pursue intimacy with Him every day.

Create a relationship with Him that supersedes any other relationship, and then watch God pave the way for you to have righteous intimacy with someone else if that's what He has planned for you. As you become intimate with God, He will help you relinquish all the junk from your previous relationships that could hinder another wholesome relationship. With Jesus as your Holy Lover, you will learn how to be a wife of valor here on earth and a bride of the Bridegroom who will come for you and welcome you to the table prepared for His beloved spouse, the church.

There is life after divorce, Baby. What better way to spend your intimate time than with the Creator of love and life, God through His Son, Jesus? Hallelujah! Now, go on about your life, living free in Jesus and glorifying the name of the Lord.

———————— ✦ ————————

Heavenly Father, *how we love You and adore You. How we appreciate You for hating our actions that are contrary to Your perfect will for our lives, but loving us enough to forgive us for them. Please help my precious sister to let go of her guilt, fear, disillusionment, and confusion, and receive all the abundance You promise to those who love You. Reassure her deep in her spirit that You have a plan for her life after divorce. Keep her heart soft and her spirit hungry for more of You. May You become the love of her life, and show her by example how to love and be loved by others. In Jesus' name, amen.*

15

I'm Confused About My Sexuality

Thelma, I have a secret I can't tell any of my Christian friends, so I'm going to talk to you if you don't mind. If you reject me, then at least I can go off and hide where you can't find me!

Okay, here it is: all my life I have had a deep affection for women. I can remember as a little girl looking at women and thinking how beautiful they were or how I'd like to be their close friend. I wanted to be near them. I've never felt that way about boys or men. I've had boyfriends, and I like them for a little while; I don't have anything against men per se. But when they want to get mushy and intimate, I feel so uncomfortable and unnatural. I just don't have a desire to be intimate with a man.

I must admit, in order to see if I was missing something, I got sexually involved with a few men in my life. But I can't stand it, Thelma. It's not my bag. I'm telling you that I have homosexual tendencies. I've had homosexual relationships.

While I'm in a relationship, I enjoy it. Women listen to me when

I talk, and they communicate to me in ways the men I've known don't. They pay attention to me and give me affection, no strings attached.

My problem, Thelma, is that I feel so guilty about my orientation and my behavior. For years I've asked myself, How did this happen when I'm a Christian? *Maybe you think I'm not, Thelma, but nobody can convince me I'm not born again. I believe in God. I love Him. I have confessed with my mouth that Jesus is Lord. I believe that He died for my sins and that God raised Him from the dead to give me eternal life. I am just as saved as any heterosexual Christian. I live in fear of my Christian so-called friends finding out and banishing me from their presence. I'm sure they'd like to banish me from God's if they could!*

I have so many questions about homosexuality. I've read books and listened to tapes. I've talked to a few of my friends who are asking some of the same questions I am, but nobody has any solid answers. I guess I don't expect you to have any answers, either. But you are such a good listener that I needed to share this with you. Maybe you can give me a little advice.

❧

First, let me thank you for feeling that you can talk to me about something so personal. You may think I'm shocked or repulsed, but I'm not. You see, my sister, Shannon, lived a lesbian lifestyle for more than thirty-five years. I've seen firsthand some of what you're dealing with.

Baby, I can imagine the confusion, guilt, condemnation, and

loneliness you have experienced. I know what it feels like to be judged and rejected because I am "different"—the color of my skin is enough to make some people hate me or at least cut a wide swath around me. Unlike you, however, I can't keep my skin color a secret! I've had to learn to deal with people's prejudice and phobias head-on. It hasn't been easy.

I tell you all this so you will know that I hear your pain and understand some of your inner turmoil. I don't know why you're the way you are, but I do know that God loves you just as He loves me.

❧

There are no easy answers. Homosexuality is so complex, nobody has been able to completely explain it. Scientists continue to do research; psychologists have their various theories; religious folks of all stripes and flavors have their opinions. I'm sure you've seen and heard it all. It has to be very confusing.

In my sister's case, she was convinced for most of her life that she was born a lesbian. She believed God made her like that. On the other hand, she always wondered whether her desire to be with women instead of men had something to do with the fact that she'd been molested by family members, Mama's boyfriends, and church members before she was even twelve years old. She says getting pregnant pushed her into a homosexual lifestyle. She took refuge in the company of women who understood and nurtured her. That's where she felt safe and loved.

But, like you, my sister felt guilty and confused in her homo-sexual relationships. She just didn't have peace in her spirit. After her daughter was born, she spent a lot of time in prayer, seeking God's mind and His will for her life and her child's. Today my sister has been out of the lesbian lifestyle for more than nine years. She says God delivered her and set her completely free. "I finally know who I am," she says, "a woman of God, sent by God, to give Him honor and glory."

Honey, I'm not going to sit here and tell you I know every-thing in God's mind on this subject. The scientific verdict isn't in yet. Mental health professionals continue to explore the various reasons a person might develop a homosexual orientation. While some things in Scripture seem clear, others don't. Educated, God-fearing theologians have various opinions and interpretations of Scripture, and sometimes they totally contradict each other. This has been true for generations. After all, in the past the Bible has been used by well-meaning believers to condemn the sick, mar-ginalize women, enslave blacks, and demonize the mentally ill. However, the Bible proclaims that homosexuality is a sin.

You have to study the Scriptures for yourself, Baby, and pray that the Holy Spirit who lives within you will show you who you are and the path He wants you on. I am convinced that when a true believer seeks God's mind without preconceived ideas and prejudices, God will reveal Himself and His will. He promises in Jeremiah 29:13 (NIV): "You will seek me and find me when you seek me with all your heart." Jesus said, "My sheep listen to my voice; I know them, and they follow me" (John 10:27 NIV). God expects us to do all things in righteousness.

So, Baby, seek God. Keep following Jesus. If you desire with all your heart to point your soul true north, He will never fail to lead you right. Trust in Him, not in yourself. He will deliver.

∽

There is no limit to God's grace. I'm glad you know where you stand as a born-again daughter of God. You have the assurance that you belong to Him, and I can tell that you love Him and want to please Him. It sounds to me, though, as if you are feeling a bit insecure about His love for you. Sweetie, you need to grab hold of His grace and wrap it around you like a warm blanket.

As my friend Barbara Johnson says, "The truth is, we are all born naked, wet, and hungry. Then things get worse. We all need grace at its best! Grace is simply knowing all about someone and loving them just the same. Jesus extends that grace to us every moment." Is that good news or what?

Sweetheart, "the LORD your God is a merciful God; he will not abandon or destroy you or forget the covenant with your forefathers, which he confirmed to them by oath" (Deut. 4:31 NIV). Do you hear that? God's mercy and faithfulness have nothing to do with *you*; they have everything to do with who *He* is and His commitment to keep His promises to you. He will *never* decide that you are just too much trouble for Him to love. No! No! No! You can count on Him to love you through thick and thin. Even if everyone else were to abandon you, God never will. *Never!*

Please understand that you cannot disappoint God. He already knows everything about you. He knows what you're going through, and He is ready, willing, and able to help you. You belong to Him. No good thing will He withhold from you. Jesus shed His blood on Calvary's cross so you could be free from sin and torment.

Girl, Romans 8:1 (NIV) jubilantly proclaims, "Therefore, there is now no condemnation for those who are in Christ Jesus." That being so, when you condemn yourself, you are out of the will of God because He, the perfect One, has not condemned you. He wants to deliver you. When you talk to yourself, you must say, "There is now no condemnation for me because God bought me at the price of His Son's life."

Baby, relinquish your attempts to change yourself, and realize that where you have no power, Jesus does. He loves you with an everlasting love, and nothing you feel or do can make Him feel any differently from that.

❧

Find support. There will always be people who don't accept us, who want us to feel like dog meat, who refuse to extend to us the grace God extends to them. What a tragedy that some of these people are our fellow believers!

My sister stopped going to church because she didn't believe she could be who she thought she was at the time. She told me, "What church was going to let somebody like I was into its squeaky clean congregation?" My sister sure felt the isolation and condemnation from her brothers and sisters in Christ that you feel now.

Girl, no matter what you hear or how you're treated, I want you to cling to one thing: you are a woman of God. You belong in His family. And believe it or not, there are Christians who will love you and support you no matter how confused you feel or how long it takes you to get clarity and peace. You've already started by talking to me. I haven't run screaming from the room, have I? I never did with my sister, either, and I never will with you.

I recently got a note from my sis that warmed the cockles of my heart. I'd like to share it with you, not only to reassure you that there are Christians who can love you unconditionally, but also to give you hope for a different future:

Sister, I want to thank you! When you finally found out about me, you never turned your back on me. I'd parade my lovers in and out of your house, and you never disrespected me or them. I'd talk badly to you sometimes and try to shut you out because I was afraid you would condemn me, but you always loved me back to you.

Granny was a jewel. She was the first in the family to know about me because she was the one we could all talk to. When I hear you talk about your sainted Granny, it makes me want to shout because she was our sainted Granny! She let me know that she did not approve of the way I was living, but she could not change me. She loved me unconditionally and many times, when I had a problem, I'd talk to her and she would always give me godly advice. She would tell me, "Baby, Granny loves you and God does, too. You're going to be all right. God's looking after you."

Those words kept me going when I was in the deepest pit! She and you were always praying for me. If you hadn't, I probably would not have made it.

❧

Live in love. Girl, I urge you to keep the faith, risk confiding in a few people you think you can trust, and let God do the rest. Most important, set your heart on loving Jesus and obeying His commands.

One time when Jesus was teaching, some Pharisees came around to try to catch Him in some kind of mistake so they could prove He didn't know what He was talking about (Mark 12:28–34 NIV). One of the teachers of the Hebrew Law asked Jesus a "trick" question—one that would be just about impossible to answer correctly.

"Of all the commandments," the teacher asked, "which is the most important?"

"The most important one," answered Jesus, "is this: 'Hear, O Israel, the Lord our God, the Lord is one. Love the Lord your

God with all your heart and with all your soul and with all your mind and with all your strength.' The second is this: 'Love your neighbor as yourself.' There is no commandment greater than these."

When the Pharisee was wise enough to admit that Jesus had answered the question well, Jesus assured the man, "You are not far from the kingdom of God."

Baby, nothing is more important than loving God and loving others. Keep your heart and soul and mind and strength set on these two things, and He will lead you forth in peace and victory.

God of grace and glory, *pour out Your power on Your children. Your power to clarify who they are and release them from confusion and bondage. God, how grateful we are that Your grace is unlimited, and Your love has no end. It boggles our minds! Thank You for loving my dear sister, for delivering her from bondage, for assuring her of Your place in Your kingdom. Please, Lord, put people in her life who will encourage her and love her as You do. Help her to trust the guidance of Your Holy Spirit inside her, and give her all the wisdom and insight she needs as she studies Your Word. Most of all, empower her to keep on loving You and others no matter what. Draw her ever closer to You, and wrap Your grace around her. In the name of Christ Jesus, amen.*

16

It's Hard to Be a Stepmother

Thelma, I think my husband's children are plotting to drive me crazy this summer! They live with their mom during the school year, so when they join their dad and me for the summer, my husband wants everything to be perfect. Last summer the visit did not go smoothly, and I'm afraid both the kids and their dad blame me for every little difficulty.

My husband doesn't want me to discipline the kids while he's at work all day or do anything that might "upset" them. He wants an atmosphere of "total love," characterized by little correcting and boundless tolerance. I can just imagine my husband saying something like, "You knew I had these children when you married me. They're good kids, and you need to show them love. That's all it will take for them to respect you. I'm their father, and disciplining them is my responsibility. You'd better not say anything to hurt their little feelings. They're only here for the summer, so just be nice to them. Just love them."

Thelma, I love my husband, and I will do everything I can to help my stepchildren have a good time here this summer. But I refuse to allow a seven- and ten-year-old to run over me the way they do when their dad's not around. They must respect me. The only way they will respect me is if I have some boundaries, set some limits, and am empowered to discipline them. What does my husband think I am, anyway? Some mean stepmother with a witch's broom beating his kids all day? Pleeease! I want what's best for all of us. I'm in this for the long haul. But I never dreamed how hard it would be to blend a previous family into our current one.

My husband and I have been married for only two years, and we're still trying to adjust to and learn about each other. Between his kids and his other family members, I'm afraid our marriage won't get the attention it needs. I've heard it said that when you marry someone, you marry his whole family. Boy, am I ever finding out how true that is! I'm at my wit's end, Thelma. What should I do?

❧

Sweetheart, I can hear how much you're struggling, trying to be a loving wife and stepmother while considering your own needs and the well-being of your marriage. I've heard from many other people about the challenges you're facing. You're not alone!

Wanting to have your spouse to yourself is understandable, but not practical. The reality is, when you marry, you *do* marry the other person's family in a way. Perhaps if you can "reframe" your situation a bit by looking at it from new angles, you'll get some perspective and hope.

❧

Don't internalize other people's issues. If you ask me, your husband sounds like a parent who feels guilty about not being with his children full time. His guilt and ambivalence lead him to compensate for his absence at the expense of throwing discipline to the wind. He's caught between pleasing you and making it up to his children. That's a tough spot to be in.

Honey, I know it's tough, but you've got to separate your husband's issues from your own. The way he's handling the whole situation really isn't about you; it's about him and his losses. Perhaps if you remember where he's coming from and validate his feelings rather than challenge everything he says, he'll be inclined to discuss your role in the children's lives more rationally and productively.

It's so important that you listen "beneath" your husband's words and actions and try to respond with wisdom and compassion to what's really going on with him. Personally, I've found that when I approach people with a sincere desire to understand their *feelings* (no matter how rigid or irrational their thoughts and behavior might be at the moment), they are usually less defensive, more inclined to talk honestly, and more willing to work with me toward a solution that feels acceptable to both of us. It's worth a try, Baby.

As for your stepkids, remember that they're trying to blend too. It may be even harder on them than on you because their daddy is married to you instead of to their mommy. There will naturally be hurt and resentment. Try not to personalize and internalize the negative things your stepchildren do and say. *It's not about you.*

I know that's hard to believe when you're in the middle of the situation, so write this down on an index card and start practicing it like a mantra: *It's not about me.* Your husband and his children have some difficult issues to work through, and doing that will take time. Don't allow yourself to become their focus; rather, encourage them to deal with their own feelings while respecting yours.

❧

Keep your eyes on the big picture. Successfully blending families can be less stressful and more fulfilling when parents focus on the big picture. That means not getting hyperfocused on the inevitable ups and downs of family life, but remembering that you are indeed together for the long haul. Many of the things that threaten to drive you crazy this summer will seem trivial down the road as your new family adjusts and matures over time. That doesn't mean your frustrations aren't real and don't need to be dealt with; but, Honey, just try to keep things in perspective. Choose your battles, and above all, keep a sense of humor. You have a choice about whether you let a seven- and ten-year-old determine your state of mind.

I can't think of a bigger picture to focus on than your family's place in the whole family of God. The most important relationship for you to forge with your husband and stepchildren is a spiritual one—one that transcends earthly family structures and rules.

Think about how Jesus defined *family*. Once when He was preaching to a crowd, someone told Him that His mother and brothers were standing nearby, wanting to speak to Him. Jesus' response was, "'Who is my mother, and who are my brothers?' Pointing to his disciples, he said, 'Here are my mother and my brothers. For whoever does the will of my Father in heaven is my brother and sister and mother'" (Matt. 12:48–50 NIV). Scripture leaves us no doubt about how much Jesus loved His mother and brothers, yet here He made the point that spiritual relationships are as important as blood ties. Jesus wanted everyone to understand that the supreme bond that people can share is a spiritual one. This is the privilege you can share with your family.

❧

Stay solution oriented. When we're frustrated and feeling stuck, it's easy to look at our whole situation as one big problem. But, Sweetie, you don't have a "situation"; you have a family. For better or for worse. If you're looking at your stepkids as problems rather than people, they'll feel it and respond accordingly.

I know of a couple who faced challenges similar to yours. The husband had four children when he married his second wife. Blending the past and the present into a new creation wasn't easy, but both husband and wife determined to keep their focus on solutions instead of problems. The wife opened her heart to the children, and together she and her husband decided how the children would be disciplined. They let it be known that the wife had the privilege to correct them when they got out of line. The wife knew, and let the children know, that she was not their mother and would never try to take the place of their mother. She was their father's wife, their stepmother. Because she loved their father, she also loved them. They could be a happy family. Even though parents and children had some rocky times getting adjusted, they were willing to do everything possible to make it work. It finally jelled. It worked.

Sweetheart, when God brought you and your husband together, He knew all about the new family He was creating. He has all the resources each of you needs to live in harmony. Make Christ the focal point and supreme authority of your family, the foundation upon which everything is decided. Remember the saying "The family that prays together stays together." Worship together, and create a spiritual heritage for generations to come. Clarify the lines of authority and responsibility for you and your husband. Let the children know the role of both parents and stepparents. Provide a regular forum for airing grievances, sharing ideas and opinions, and making family decisions, showing appreciation for each person's contributions to the family. Heartfelt harmony, peace, and order require clear, direct, and convincing communication.

Family relationships should be subservient to our relationship with God. He made the perfect family in Adam and Eve. He desired that they should never have problems or have to make the kind of decisions we must make today. After the fall of humankind in the Garden, the perfect family was destroyed. Separation, divorce, children out of wedlock, and remarriage became reality. But in all of this, our loving and gracious God has a plan for children and families to thrive. Your desire to form a happy family goes a long way in blending bloodlines and soul ties together. You can do it!

Father, *the family was Your first institution. You knew that people needed each other to survive on this earth. Thank You for Your grace that continues to work in families today. No matter how complex our relationships, You offer solutions and hope. Help my sister, dear Lord, to lean on You alone as she strives to be the loving wife and stepmother You have ordained her to be. Give her total access to Your perfect wisdom and Your unfailing love. In our human families, You have given us a glimpse of what being a part of Your heavenly family is like. You are the Father; we are the children. You want what's best for us, and we want to please You. Thank You for adopting us into the family of God and blending us with Your chosen people. Help us to love our family members the way You love Your children. In Your Son's name, amen.*

17

I Have a Problem with Anger

Thelma, I have a terrible temper. I live in anger mode almost all the time. Everything pushes my buttons.

For example, the other day I was stopped at a red light. When the signal changed to green, I wasn't paying attention. The woman in the car behind me honked, and that ticked me off. I just stopped in the middle of the turn, hoping she would hit me so I'd have a reason to tell her off to her face. I can't believe I got so mad at a stranger that I was willing to risk causing an accident!

I can hardly control my irritation when I'm standing in line at the grocery store, watching as the slow, methodical cashier takes her time ringing up the purchases while talking to the customer about nothing. She's not paid to talk; she's paid to check people out. She needs to cut out the yackety-yak and get people out of there!

When people call me on the telephone at work and talk nasty to me, I think I have a right to get nasty with them too. I don't have to take that! I've been reprimanded at work for my temper, but I just can't help it. Thelma, I get so sick of people and all their demands. I'm not going to be their punching bag.

It's no better at home. As soon as I walk into the house after work, there's somebody telling me what happened at school or some other junk that I'd just as soon not hear right then, thank you very much. Give me a break! I just walked in the door. I'm tired. I don't feel like being leaped on by my kids.

I hate to admit it, Thelma, but I know my constant anger and irritability are my problem. Every day I tell myself that I won't get mad, but the minute things don't go my way, I'm angry again. I feel that I don't have any control over it. I know other people suffer because of my bad temper. Do you have any suggestions on how I can deal with this rage inside me?

◈

I sure do, Sugar. (Now don't get mad at me for calling you Sugar. Remember, I'm from the South.) May I call you Sugar? Good.

Anger is a natural emotion. We are all born with the capacity to get angry. Watch what happens in a newborn baby when she doesn't get something she wants! Anger is a defensive emotional technique that can be used for or against us. It can help us be sensitive to certain areas in our lives that need attention, but we can abuse the emotion and use it for manipulation or aggression. Anger itself is not good or bad, and being anger-free is neither realistic nor desirable.

Baby, I get angry too. You bet I do. Some days, everything

and everyone threatens to get on my last nerve! But I've learned a few things about managing my anger that I hope will help you.

❧

Analyze your anger. When I start seething inside, I've learned to ask myself a few questions: *What's really going on here? What am I afraid of? How important is it really?*

The truth is, nobody can *make* you mad. Eleanor Roosevelt once said, "No one can make you feel inferior without your consent." Getting mad is a decision that you make in response to a particular stressor.

Next time you start feeling mad, *stop.* (No, this is not impossible.) You do not *have* to react in the heat of the moment; you can usually remove yourself from the situation, even from the room, until you have a few sane moments to make a conscious choice about how to respond. Pull away and think about what's really going on. Is your anger a direct result of a real, specific wrong done directly to you by another person? If it is, then your anger can be a helpful signal that something needs to be addressed or a relationship needs to be improved. God doesn't expect us to be doormats or punching bags. Sometimes our anger is legitimate and can motivate us to find creative and effective solutions to real problems.

Sometimes, however, we get mad just because we're tired. Or hungry. Maybe your blood sugar was off kilter when that lady honked at you! Did the last person you got mad at hurt you intentionally, or were you just in the wrong place at the wrong time? Tuning in to the various factors that can contribute to your bad temper can really help you keep things in perspective. Girl, sometimes getting mad just ain't necessary!

People stay in anger mode for a number of reasons. What are your reasons? If you're like me, you get the most angry when you don't feel that you're in control of something. I've found that fear often resides underneath my feelings of anger. When I feel threatened in some way, I get mad. That's a natural human defense mechanism. Think about that when you get angry. Are you afraid of losing something you have or not getting something you want? When we recognize the fear beneath our anger, we can take steps to feel safe, set boundaries, and ask God for wise direction. When the perceived threat is removed, the anger often melts away.

Finally, ask yourself if what you're angry about is worth the emotional investment you're making in staying mad. Have you ever thought about the amount of energy it takes to get angry and stay that way? (I'm sure you have.) The energy of anger causes your body to do strange things. Muscles tighten, eyes squint and get red, skin color changes, teeth grit, head hurts, heart beats irregularly, blood vessels constrict, stomach gets upset, veins pop out, voice tone gets high; in other words, your entire body begins to shake, rattle, and roll as it screams, "HELP! I'M HAVING A FIT!" Girl, can you really afford to let your body go through all those gyrations on a daily basis? Is it really worth it?

Sometimes, it certainly is. After all, Scripture has a whole lot to say about God's wrath because of sin; God is no namby-pamby pushover when it comes to people's hearts. He forgives, but He does not excuse wickedness. He doesn't expect us to sweep sin under the table, either. God, enfleshed in Jesus, got angry plenty of times when anger was the appropriate response to a situation. When people disrespected His Father, were cruel to each other, lorded it over others, or ran slipshod over truth, He got mad. But He wasn't abusive in His anger, nor did He seek retaliation. He was angry, but He did not sin. He expects the same of us (Eph. 4:26).

The first step toward managing your temper is to take a good look at yourself and analyze the underlying cause of your anger. You are the only one who can determine what's really going on. Ask God for the courage to examine yourself honestly. I think you'll find that the flaw usually is not in other people; it's in you. And that's good news, Baby, because you and God can *do* something about *you*.

❧

Develop empathy. Have you ever been at a signal light or a stop sign and the cars in front of you were hesitating to move? You can't tell me you've never in your life honked at someone. How would you feel if that person had stopped in the middle of the street and you had hit him? I guess that would have made you mad, too, Sugar.

Have you ever snapped at someone when you didn't feel good, or when you were up all night with a sick kid, or when you were worried about something totally unrelated to the task or person in front of you? When someone is being "nasty" to you, is it really about you? Do you *have* to react? Or can you just let him have his feelings and move out of his line of fire?

Tell me, how would you feel if your family ignored you when you walked into the house after work? If they acted like you were invisible, insignificant? That would not just make you mad; it would hurt your feelings.

My point is, try to put yourself in other people's shoes. What might your kids be thinking and feeling when you come home from work? "Here's Mama. She can fix anything. She knows everything. She must be happy to see us because we're happy to see her." If you need to wind down when you first get home, just calmly ask your family to let you sit down for fifteen minutes; then you will be ready to listen to the day's stories and dish out love as I know you want to do. You don't need to get angry. Just communicate with them.

Most important, stop being so arrogant. (I know, now I *really* made you mad!) Seriously, meditate on Paul's words in Romans 2:1 (NIV): "You, therefore, have no excuse, you who pass judgment on someone else, for at whatever point you judge the other, you are condemning yourself, because you who pass judgment do the same things."

Baby, we're all in this earthbound boat together. Until we're released into the heavenly realm where we'll all be perfect, we'll continue to hurt each other, intentionally and unintentionally. We all get on each other's nerves. We all have bad days and make mistakes. Cut other people some slack, just as you want them to do for you. Memorize these words from the apostle James, and ask God to bring them to your mind when you start to heat up: "My dear brothers, take note of this: Everyone should be quick to listen, slow to speak and slow to become angry, for man's anger does not bring about the righteous life that God desires" (James 1:19–20 NIV).

What do you *really* want, Sugar? To lay into the people who irritate you, or to become more like Jesus? You have a choice.

❧

Act "as if." Girl, you have practiced being angry for a long time. Sounds to me as if it's become a bad habit. The good news is, all habits can be changed. The catch is that the person who changes has to *want* to change. Baby, I think you do!

Whenever you feel yourself getting angry, force yourself to stop and pray. Ask God to help you determine why you get angry so quickly. Then challenge the way you're thinking about the situation. Change the way you talk to yourself about it, and then act as if your thinking has already changed. Say something like, "I am calm. I am staying calm. With God's help, I am handling this. This is working out for me." Talking to yourself with affir-

mations can help you break your habit of getting angry and flying off the handle.

Facial expressions can also make a difference in how you deal with anger. People who smile often are less likely to get angry. When you smile, endorphins are secreted in your brain, creating a more positive response in your body than when you frown. People who frown more than they smile are more likely to be upset all the time. Even people who don't frown much are more susceptible to negative responses than those who smile. So smile more. Act as if you're happy, and you probably will be!

It makes sense to me to channel the negative energy it takes to get angry in a more positive direction. Use that same energy to think positively, talk to yourself pleasantly, and look happy. Just try this for twenty-one days, and see what happens: It takes at least three weeks to make or break a habit. You can do it!

Sugar, you don't have to live in anger mode all the time. You have a choice. Learn to correctly identify the source of your anger, realize you're not that different from the people you think "make" you mad, and be obedient to what you know is right. Realize that self-control is possible when you allow God to rule in your heart.

Dear Jesus, *You have all the right in the world to be angry with us for all the things we do that displease You. We ignore You, don't talk* to You, act as if we think You owe us something, and You still don't pay us back what we deserve. Thank You! Father, by the power of Your Holy Spirit within us, enable us to imitate You in this area of anger management. Show us that we can be honest about all our feelings, including anger, without sinning against You or others. Please help this dear daughter of Yours to channel her negative energy in a positive direction so that when she feels angry, it will work for her rather than against her. Please take control of her emotions and her tongue, and replace her rage with peace and love. In the name of Jesus we pray, amen.

18

I Have Too Much to Do and Too Little Time

There are simply not enough hours in the day, Thelma. I don't have nearly the time to do everything I need and want to do. By the time I get up, fix breakfast, get my family off to school and work, get my own workday planned, get to appointments on time, wash, iron, clean, cook, sew, take care of everyone—Thelma, my blood pressure soars just thinking about all the stuff I have to do!

One thing is sure, I've discovered that I'm not Superwoman. My body gets worn out, and my attitude goes down the tubes. I can be busy doing something in the kitchen, and my husband will ask me to bring him a glass of water. He's got two good hands and legs. Sometimes I snap at him, "Get your own water! Can't you see I'm busy?" Then I feel bad because of the way I talked to him. He doesn't seem to get upset with me, but why can't he see I'm busy and not even ask me to do stuff for him?

Getting people to help me at home is like pulling eyeteeth. When I do laundry, you'd think they wouldn't mind folding the clothes and putting them away. Most of the clothes are theirs anyway. But do you think they ask me if I need any help? Not on your life. They just sit there watching TV while I'm folding, walking back and forth putting their stuff in their closets and drawers, and act as if they don't see me. They just think I'm there to help them. *When I ask them to pitch in, they look at me as if I asked them to climb Mount Everest. Well, sometimes they move quickly and help. But most of the time they have excuses. If I don't stay on them, they wait until I get mad and start screaming at them before they make an effort to pitch in.*

And I have another problem. My friends call me all the time telling me their business and asking for my help. I don't have time to talk to them for hours on the phone, but I'm afraid that if I tell them I can't talk, they'll get upset with me. One of my good friends even stops by my house several times a week. After she leaves, I've got to work double-time to do everything I could have done while she was there.

Something's got to give, Thelma. I just can't take this pace anymore. I can't meet everyone's expectations and keep my sanity. Do you have these problems? How do you manage your time?

❧

Oh, Sweetheart, how your words remind me of myself in those years of child rearing and husband taming. I know exactly how you feel and what you're going through. I was able to solve some of the problems you've described, but I think you've already identified your biggest dilemma: you can't meet everyone's expectations. You're right about that! And that's what you have to come to terms with in order to change your life for the better.

❦

Ask for what you need. Why not call a family meeting and gently, with kindness, tell the family how you feel about needing more help at home? You may even ask them what chores they would prefer. Let them know that if everyone pitches in and helps, it will not be hard on any one person.

In our house, we found that having specific chores assigned to each individual was better than having people rotate or pitch in when the mood struck them (which it never did). If a certain job did not get done, we held one person responsible. Of course, there were times when someone needed to trade out or help someone else do his chores, but all in all it worked out pretty well. Our son got to the point that he didn't want to mow the lawn anymore. That was all right with us as long as it got cut. He used some of his allowance and work money to pay for the yard. Not a problem. I just wanted the yard mowed, and my son knew it was his responsibility.

Our daughter discovered it was best to clean up the kitchen as soon as we finished the evening meal. That was easier than being awakened at 2:00 A.M. by a crazy mother because the dishes were still in the sink. In the mornings, we required everyone to clean up after himself. We were all trying to get out of the house on time.

Sometimes a husband feels that if a woman is in the house, he should not have to do much. It's a man thang! And it's hard teaching an old dog new tricks. In our family, we had to accept that Daddy's job was to keep up the cars and the lawn equipment, fix stuff around the house, and supervise. Asking him to do any housework was, well, ineffective. Some things you just can't change. But the truth is, he was helping a lot because seldom did we get into a dirty car or run out of gas for the lawn mower or have to hire a handyman. We really couldn't complain. Most of the time, everything worked out all right. Each of us played a part and appreciated the others' contributions.

So, Baby, be proactive. Rather than being passive, manipulative, or angry, work on communicating clearly with your family members. Be forthright about what you want and need, and be willing to listen and negotiate about what each person can contribute to the smooth running of the household. Things can change. Get started.

❧

Practice setting boundaries. Now, about your friends and loved ones who call or drop by unannounced. You may need to do the same thing with them as you'll do with the people inside your house. When that person calls you on the phone for a two-hour conversation about stuff you can't do anything about, learn how to gracefully bow out. You might say something like, "Friend, I know you need to talk about this, and I want to talk with you.

A convenient time for me to talk for a while is between 9:30 and 10:00 tonight. I can listen better then. Right now I have so much to do and a short time to do it in. Girl, I know you can understand that. Call me back when I can talk to you without distraction and interruption. I'll look forward to it!"

Guess what? A lot of times that person will find someone else who will listen to her right then, and she won't call you back at all. Many people just need a listening ear when they want it, not at your convenience. If your friend doesn't call you back, don't get upset. Call it success. You kindly set some boundaries that worked for you without neglecting your responsibility to care for your friend.

Believe it or not, the person who stops by can be even easier to deal with than the person on the phone. Unless you've invited someone over, you have no obligation to just sit and allow her to alter your plans for the day. If you're like me, you can continue working while your friend is at your house. When someone stops by my house unannounced, I tell her that I appreciate her stopping. I can talk for a minute, but then I'll have to get back to a project I'm working on. If she says, "I just want to talk," often I'll ask, "Do you mind me working while you're talking?" What else is she going to say but yes?

You can sense if someone really needs your undivided attention or if she just wants to yak. When I've explained to my uninvited guest what I need to do, asked permission to continue, given her some attention but still accomplished what I needed to do, then both of us can be happy. I have not been rude to her; I've simply been straightforward.

Baby, it's *okay* to make some of the decisions about how and when you give to the people you love. Sure, there are times when a friend or loved one is in crisis, and God may call you to be there for that person, even if it means not getting all your work done. But your life doesn't have to be a revolving door for people in need at the expense of the other things God has called you to do.

Consider Jesus' example: He certainly laid down His life for people on a daily basis; but He also pulled away from the crowds in order to pray and spend time alone (Mark 1:35; Luke 5:16). He didn't always give people what they wanted when they wanted it. He didn't always stay when people wanted Him to or heal when people asked Him to. He let His Father determine His priorities, and He followed the Father's agenda regardless of people's opinions. "My food," said Jesus, "is to do the will of him who sent me and to finish his work" (John 4:34 NIV).

❧

Let God set your priorities. If you're as much like me as it seems, you probably give yourself to a lot of other things besides your friends and family. You probably belong to organizations that demand a lot of your time; you probably teach Sunday school or volunteer for one too many committees.

Girl, I was once a member of so many organizations that I

was in a meeting almost every day or night of the week. I started getting a headache on the way to some of those meetings. When I asked myself why I was so involved, two answers came to mind without my permission: (1) I couldn't say no, and (2) I had a big ego. Yes, ego. I enjoyed seeing my name on the stationery of prestigious organizations. But, Baby, they were draining me dry. I had little time for my family, for the things I enjoyed doing, and for the commitments God was actually calling me to make. It was time to make some wiser choices.

I spent time in prayer, evaluating what each group was doing and how it benefited me or I benefited it. It didn't take long to realize that the cost-benefit ratio was way out of line in several cases. So, I resigned from all the organizations and committees and boards except three. I kept my professional association with the local and national chapters of the National Speakers Association. I remained the volunteer chair of the Bethlehem Foundation, a charitable organization that helps thousands of people each year with food, clothing, rent, utilities, and medical necessities. And I continued my church work as a Sunday school teacher, and as a member of the choir and Board of Trustees. That was it. That was plenty.

Girl, my stress level went down at least five hundred degrees! It's amazing how much energy and time you can spend doing stuff for various causes that have little to do with God's causes for *you*. When you have poor boundaries, an exaggerated sense of personal responsibility, and a chubby ego, it's easy to let other people's agendas become your agenda. It happens so subtly that you may not recognize it until you're sucked in and drained dry. So, Baby, be alert and aware, and constantly consult God your Father so you won't get trapped by the time snatchers that He hasn't put on your list.

I try to live by the wisdom in Ecclesiastes:

> There is a time for everything,
> and a season for every activity under heaven:
> a time to be born and a time to die,
> a time to plant and a time to uproot,
> a time to kill and a time to heal,
> a time to tear down and a time to build,
> a time to weep and a time to laugh,
> a time to mourn and a time to dance,
> a time to scatter stones and a time to gather them,
> a time to embrace and a time to refrain,
> a time to search and a time to give up,
> a time to keep and time to throw away,
> a time to tear and a time to mend,
> a time to be silent and a time to speak,
> a time to love and a time to hate,
> a time for war and a time for peace. (3:1–8 NIV)

My daily prayer is, "Lord, open the doors I need to walk through today. Close the doors I don't. Get people out of my way that I don't need to talk to today, and put those in my path that I do. And, Lord, please don't let me waste Your time!"

Why don't you adopt a prayer like that? Trusting God to help you use your time wisely will go a long way toward your success.

———————— ✦ ————————

Dear Father, *thank You for Your infinite wisdom, Your boundless patience, and Your matchless grace. We are so grateful that Your agenda for us fits us perfectly. You already know exactly how You want us to spend our time and resources, and You're more than willing to tell us if only we'll consult You! Lord, reassure my sister that You are a God of grace, not of pressure. Thank You for showing us by example that we are not meant to do everything for everyone all the time. You know what everyone needs, and You are in charge of meeting these needs. Remind us to ask You first before we volunteer to be "on call" twenty-four hours a day because our ego is convinced that no one can live without us. Humble us to reach out for help when we need it. Help my friend, Lord, to say NO when You lead her so that her YES can be wholehearted and full of joy. In Your Son's holy name, amen.*

19

I Don't Believe God Is Still Working in the World Today

Thelma, when I look around me at the world today, it's really hard for me to believe that God is still at work. When I turn on the news, I see nothing but disaster everywhere.

Just last week there was another earthquake that killed thousands of people. Hurricanes are battering the shorelines of some of the most beautiful beaches in the world. Flood and fire and drought abound.

AIDS and HIV still have no cure, and diseases like tuberculosis that once were under control are becoming epidemics again. Cancer destroys people of all ages. Psychologists say that depression is the number one ailment among women. There seems to me to be more broken people today than ever before.

People in other countries are being killed and forced out of the lands and homes they have built with their blood, sweat, and tears. People are starving to death because of corrupt governments and failed crops. People are paying more attention to saving trees and whales than to helping people in need.

Little babies are being abandoned by the hundreds. Many others are being beaten and neglected, even in my own city, by their own parents! I never thought I'd see the day when my children would not be able to play in the yard without someone watching over them like a hawk. I read that in one of the nation's grocery stores, a mother turned around to look at a package of meat. When she turned back, her little girl was missing. The child was found in the men's bathroom, naked, with her half-shaved head in the toilet. Thank God, she was revived and saved. But tell me, just where was God when all this was going on?

People are being killed by stray bullets intended for somebody else. Arsonists are setting fires to houses of God and homes where Christians reside. Teenagers who profess Jesus as Savior are being shot down like mad dogs. Taxi drivers are shot because they trust passengers. And I just read about a passenger who was abducted and raped by a taxi driver!

Older people are being mistreated and swindled out of their hard-earned money. Institutions that were once rock solid are being infiltrated by embezzlers. Electronic crime is on the rise. Scammers and hackers are on a rampage. The Internet is serving up pornography with a few keystrokes.

The nation's prisons are overloaded with young people mostly between the ages of seventeen and thirty-seven. Justice seems to be on the side of the person with the fattest pocketbook. There are people in the government who can get away with anything and poor people who get the book thrown at them for minor misdemeanors.

The cost of living continues to rise while the value of the dollar decreases. Even though some people actually have more than they've ever had in their lives, the rich keep getting richer and the poor keep getting poorer. If things keep going in this direction, the difference between the haves and the have-nots will be so distinguishable that a whole new class system will emerge.

Gang wars are raging. Guns are everywhere. Airplanes are falling out of the sky. Cruise ships are colliding. Innocent people are being killed by drunk drivers every minute. Children are being run over.

I'm sick of people talking about family values when they are the very ones messing up in their own families. The preacher, politician, teacher, and school superintendent talk about creating a happy and secure atmosphere for our children to thrive in at home and in the community, and then they end up on television for some stupid mistake they've made.

Thelma, the world is going to Hades in a handbasket. And God doesn't seem to care.

❧

Girl, you're right about the mess this world is in. I can't argue with you; thangs ain't purty. In fact, they haven't been for a looong time.

Many generations before our time, the psalmist David lamented,

> Help, LORD, for the godly are no more;
>> the faithful have vanished from among men . . .
> The wicked freely strut about
>> when what is vile is honored among men. (Ps. 12:1, 8 NIV)

He went on to say,

> The LORD looks down from heaven on the sons of men
> to see if there are any who understand,
>> any who seek God.
> All have turned aside,
>> they have together become corrupt;
> there is no one who does good,
>> not even one. (Ps: 14:2–3 NIV)

The prophet Habakkuk felt a lot like you do right now:

> How long, O LORD, must I call for help,
>> but you do not listen?
> Or cry out to you, "Violence!"
>> but you do not save?
> Why do you make me look at injustice?
>> Why do you tolerate wrong?
> Destruction and violence are before me;
>> there is strife, and conflict abounds. (Hab. 1:2–3 NIV)

Sound familiar?

Sister, this sin-sick world ain't gonna get any better. This is the enemy's domain until Jesus returns in justice and glory. But I know it's tough. Even righteous believers such as David, Habakkuk, you, and me can get discouraged in the midst of all the evil and destruction that surrounds us. But we don't ever have to lose our faith in God's goodness or His mighty work on our behalf.

❧

Remember who God is. The sorrowful things going on in the world are the work not of God but of the enemy, the devil. We live in a fallen world where corruption and carnality are the norm. Even people who believe in Jesus and who have committed their whole lives to Him to rule and guide have a hard time getting in line with right.

When devastation occurs, I can imagine God crying over His children just as He rejoices over us when we exalt Him. For every child who is missing, God grieves. For every older person who is mistreated and every spouse who is battered, God grieves. God hates sin. He cares when we have been sinned against, and Jesus knows from experience what it feels like to be sinned against.

When you find yourself questioning the integrity or goodness of God, pick up your Bible and search for the truth. See for yourself what God's Word has to say about the goodness and greatness of the Almighty. I'm reminded of a few words to a song that asks, "Does Jesus care . . . Oh yes, He cares. His heart is touched with our grief. When the world goes weary, the long night dreary, I know my Savior cares."

Baby, what is going on in the world is no surprise to Jesus. Remember, He was the One who said, "I have told you these things, so that in me you may have peace. In this world you will have trouble. But take heart! I have overcome the world" (John 16:33 NIV).

✏

Change your focus. Many excellent, successful, wonderful, exciting happenings in the world today don't make the front page of the newspaper or the six o'clock news. After all, great things and wonderful people are not sensational enough to sell papers. Yet they are actually the everyday occurrences that we miss because we believe that what the media tell us is the whole truth and nothing but the truth.

The apostle Paul told his fellow believers, "Whatever is true, whatever is noble, whatever is right, whatever is pure, whatever is lovely, whatever is admirable—if anything is excellent or praiseworthy—think about such things . . . And the God of peace will be with you" (Phil. 4:8–9 NIV).

Sweetie, you probably spent a lot of time and energy listing for me all the trouble and sorrow you see in your world. I encourage you to spend even more time and energy thinking about what is good and right—especially in your life. You get to choose what you focus on. I suggest that you don't read the newspaper or watch the evening news for a while. Believe me, you won't miss anything that won't still be there when you tune in again! Make a decision to change your focus from what's wrong to what's right. Then thank God for those things. Thank God every day, again and again and again, that He has already overcome evil by dying and rising again in the person of His Son, Jesus. Establish a new habit for yourself: looking for the good instead of the bad. It's there, Baby. Open your eyes.

❧

Don't overlook the evidence of God at work. The place you're in right now reminds me of something that came up for one of my children when she was nearly ten years old. My daughter, Vikki, announced to me in an adult fashion, "Mama, I don't think the Lord is still working in the world today."

"Whaaat?" I asked.

Vikki repeated her position.

My mouth was open, but no words came out. What do you say to something like this when you think your child has received Jesus Christ as Savior and accepted that God is Ruler over all? The only thing I could say was, "Yes, He is, Girl!"

Vikki's reply, "Well, I just don't think He is."

Her comments called for an urgent talk with God. I asked Him to prove to my daughter that He is still working in the world. That He cares and that He's in control of everything.

Several days after I prayed, Vikki hurried into our bedroom very early one morning and frantically told us to come quickly and see what had happened to Granny. As soon as I got to Granny's room and saw her twisted mouth and limp arms, I knew what had happened. She'd had a stroke.

I immediately called our family doctor and asked him to

come by on his way to the office. When he got there, he confirmed what I suspected. It was serious. He said Granny would never again be able to talk, walk, swallow, or move without help. He told me that I had to make a decision about what to do with her because I could not take care of her at home.

No! No! No! This couldn't be happening. She was fine last night when she went to bed!

I was more than a little miffed with God. I had asked Him to please let me know before He took Granny so I could prepare. I'd even asked Him to take me before He took her because I did not think I'd be able to live without her. Now He'd put me in the situation of having to consider sending her to a nursing home, something I'd promised her I'd never do. I was hacked off.

After I telephoned family members and a few friends, I passed by our daughter's bedroom. There on her knees was Vikki, praying. I looked, but I didn't disturb her. When she finished, she came into the kitchen and said, with a glow of peace and contentment on her face, "Mama, Granny's going to be just fine." I wanted to believe that, but I don't think I did.

Family and friends came to help decide the fate of Granny while she lay asleep in her bedroom. At one o'clock in the afternoon, there came a sound from Granny's room. "Thelma Baby, why d'ya let me sleep so long? I'm so hungry I don't know what to do."

It was Granny—talking, walking, fully recovered! God had healed her according to the faith of a girl not yet ten years old.

Ever since that day, my Vikki and my whole family have been convinced, without a shadow of a doubt, that God is working in the world today. God proved that He is in control of life and death, sickness and health. His word is more powerful than any doctor's.

In every situation, whether climatic or disastrous, dangerous or insane, disappointing or debilitating, cruel or mean, good or bad, Jesus is Lord. And, Sister, He's coming back to establish His righteous kingdom on earth. Satan may be busy in the world today, but God almighty reigns in eternity. Hallelujah!

O God in heaven, *sometimes it looks as if You have forsaken this old sin-sick world. It seems that You've gone on vacation and just removed Your hand from us. But in our hearts, we know that's not true. You promised never to leave us or forsake us. You cannot lie. When we get out of sorts and begin to doubt Your presence or question Your concern for us, please remind us, as You did Vikki, that You are still in control of the universe today. Remind us that You've got the whole world in Your hands and nobody can pluck it out. And, Lord, thank You that when we have these doubts and fears, You don't fall off Your throne or make us do one thousand push-ups and beat us over the head with our own nonsense. You simply love us anyway and cover us with your grace and mercy. What a mighty God You are, the One who rules earth and heaven! Amen.*

God Will Make a Way

From Genesis to Revelation the Bible overflows with promises that God made to His people. At the age of fifty-five, Thelma Wells began a careful study of some of these promises.

With lively insight and humor that make her one of the most sought after speakers in the country, Thelma relates God's promises to the challenges we face every day in this inspiring devotional.

0-7852-7542-8 • hardcover
$14.99 • 168 pages

What's Going on Lord?

Personal examples, practical strategies, and Bible promises are woven together to encourage women to affirm that God is working in their everyday lives. An inspirational book written with warmth and humor by one of the featured speakers for the Women of Faith conferences.

0-7852-7030-2 • hardcover
$14.99 • 168 pages

About the Author

Thelma Wells is president of A Woman of God Ministries in Dallas, Texas where she mentors women in the ways of Christ. She has a masters in pastoral ministry and is the author of several popular books, including *What's Going on Lord* and *God Will Make a Way*. She is a key speaker for the Women of Faith® Conferences where she has ministered to nearly two million women.